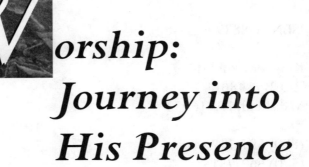

# Worship: Journey into His Presence

by Dr. Robert Webber

D1366837

**Kingdom** ™
publishing
Mansfield, PA

ISBN: 1-883906-31-8

Kingdom Publishing
P.O. Box 486
Mansfield, PA  16933

(800) 597-1123
(570) 662-7515

http://www.kingdompub.com
email = info@kingdompub.com

# *orship: Journey into His Presence*

# *reface*

My aim in writing *Worship: Journey into His Presence* has been to develop how God becomes present in our lives and to reflect on how we are to respond to the presence of God.

I am aware that Biblical thought always begins with God. It is always God who initiates a relationship with us. Throughout history God has reached out again and again to save us, to heal us, to restore us, and to give us life abundant. We know that His intervention has not ended. God continues to be present to us, to say to us individually as well as to the whole community, "I made you for myself; I want my glory to be shown in you. Meet me now and be transformed by my presence."

But how do we gain entrance to His presence? It is in the act of worship that God's most intense presence occurs. God gathers us, God speaks to us, God acts upon us, and we go forth into the world with God's presence to love and serve God in all of our ways.

The experience of God's presence in worship is not a static form — a cold, mechanical ritual we go through; nor is the presence of God a mere exercise of the mind — a thought process in which we acquire certain doctrines about God. True worship is a journey into the Presence. It is a relationship with the divine. Its goal is not so much the gaining of information about God, but *gaining God.* It is not a union in

5

which our individual personality is lost into some kind of divine abyss, but a union with the God who is wholly other yet one of us. It is a union that ignites our personality and sets it on fire with all that it means to have been created in the image of God.

Because worship is a journey, a progression into God's presence, I want to explore with you the themes of journey and presence. I want, as much as is possible, to explain the personal experiential dimension of the presence of God. He created each of us; and when we fell away into sin, He made the unprecedented move to become one of us, to die in our place to overthrow the powers of evil, and to be resurrected for our healing and restoration.

The organizing principle that ignites this whole book is the story of Cleopas and his companion, told in Luke 24:13-53. I recommend that you read this passage before you continue reading this book.

# reparation for the Journey

*Two of them were going to a village called Emmaus (Luke 24:13).*

There have been events in my life that fill me with awe and wonder because they contain both an element of surprise and a humbling assurance of a personal God. One such event occurred in 1968. I'd like to share the story with you in preparation for our journey together.

> *I was teaching at a seminary in the Midwest while working on my doctoral degree. Certain things had happened that made me feel uncomfortable with the prospect of spending my life at this seminary, but since I had a family to support and teaching positions were hard to get, I didn't feel I had a choice.*
>
> *In February, contracts for the next year were passed out, and the faculty members were asked to sign and return our contracts by early March. I remember looking and looking at my contract and hearing a voice inside me say, "Don't sign the contract, Bob. This is not the place for you." No sooner did I hear this voice than a different voice chimed in saying, "Don't be stupid! It's a good job. Think of your family!"*

7

*The voices didn't stop. In fact, this internal dialogue went on for the best part of the month. The deadline loomed closer and closer, but I still had no sense of resolution. That fateful day finally arrived when the contracts were due, and I pulled the document out of my pocket yet again. It seemed as though the voices within me were nearly shouting at one another as I opened the contract and picked up a pen. Ignoring the voices, I placed the pen on the dotted line and began to sign my name. I had only finished the "R" for my first name when I threw the pen down, snatched up the contract, and went home.*

*I did nothing more for two days. Then I asked my young family, "Do you know what this means? I'm giving up a good job, and I have no idea where we are going to live or what we are going to do. Are you willing to take the risk?"*

*Their answer was a confident "Yes!" Peace descended on my heart.*

*That very night, the phone rang. "Bob," said the person on the other line, "I've been trying to call you for two weeks. Where have you been?"*

*"Right here," I answered, puzzled. "I haven't gone anyplace. Who's calling?"*

*"I chair the theology department at Wheaton College, and we're looking for a person to fill a new vacancy. I've been trying to catch you before you signed your contract for next year. First of all, are you available; and secondly, are you interested in being considered for the job?"*

*Wow! In order to fully appreciate my relief at this moment, you must also know that eight years earlier — when someone had asked me what I wanted to do with my life — I had answered, "I want to teach at Wheaton College!" I was very conscious of God acting on my behalf, making His presence clearly evident at a moment in my life when I was in great need.*

*When I was interviewed at Wheaton, I said, "If you give me this position, I'll stay here for the rest of my life." At the time of this writing I have spent 30 years at Wheaton.*

You may have a similar story that you also delight in, one that brings praise to God and shows how He is at work in our lives. The Bible — especially the New Testament — is full of wonderful stories of how God shows up in the lives of His people. Sharing our testimony-stories with others deepens their faith (and ours) in God's loving provision and His sovereign power. This is why the sharing of stories is a centuries-old, enduring practice of the Church.

\*　　\*　　\*　　\*　　\*　　\*

In the historic tradition of worship, there has been a service each year on the eve of Easter that is called the Great Paschal Vigil. During this service, scriptures are read that teach the story of faith from creation and the fall; to the covenant with Israel; then the coming of John the Baptist; the story of Mary; the birth of Jesus and His death; and, finally, His glorious resurrection. These readings cover the full, historical scope of salvation, thrusting us into an active, living, breathing presence of faith that demands our total involvement.

During the time of the Early Church, the Vigil readings were extensive. The reader began at dusk and ended at the crack of dawn. By contrast, there are many churches today that continue the Paschal Vigil, but set aside only an hour or so for the readings!

I've personally been involved in the reading portion of the Vigil service a number of times and each time have enjoyed hearing the old, old story again. On one occasion after the readings, a mother came to me and excitedly said: "Bob, while the readings were going on my nine-year-old daughter turned to me with a sparkle in her eye and said: 'Mommy, don't you just love those stories?'" We were both amazed that a nine-year-old was listening with such involvement and intense appreciation; however, the truth is that we all love stories.

Stories have always been — and still are — a part of every culture. We love stories and storytellers because they touch not only our minds, but our hearts as well. One reason we love the Gospels is because they are full of stories. The stories are almost always about Jesus: Jesus turns water into wine; Jesus heals the sick; Jesus encounters people, such as the Pharisees, and makes His point through teaching stories (called parables) and illustrations. In His time, Jesus was the great storyteller; and, of course, there were numerous stories to be told about Jesus. Consequently, when we enter into the venues of the Early Church, we find many individuals who have a story to tell about Jesus, and the people loved to hear those stories again and again. Just imagine Peter telling stories about his experience with Jesus. I can see someone in the crowd calling out to Peter, "Hey, Peter, tell us the story of Jesus calming the waters." Peter smiles and says, "I'd love to; it's one of my favorites!"

10

Before we develop this further, let's define our terms. For many people, a *story* implies fiction; and although the parables are a fictional form, the other stories are biographical. They are short chunks of history. Because in Bible times few people were literate, information was largely passed on by word of mouth; so our definition of story here is *an oral account of something that really happened.*

Not only did people look to Peter for stories about Jesus, but to any and all of the other eyewitnesses. The Apostles and the disciples of Jesus were not only followers of Jesus, but seasoned storytellers. They also were itinerant storytellers — going from place to place to tell their stories to eager and expectant audiences.

After the resurrection and ascension events, these storytellers were in great demand as they traveled from city to city. People would meet in the street and say, "Guess who's going to be at the assembly this Sabbath. Peter is coming! I can't wait to hear his stories!" The people wanted to hear these stories because through them they felt as though they got a little piece of Jesus.

One of the greatest stories of post-resurrection times is the story of Cleopas and his companion on the road to Emmaus. Cleopas and his companion (perhaps his wife?) were likely great storytellers, and it's easy to picture them traveling from church to church all over Palestine and beyond. Wherever they journeyed, they captured the attention of thousands of people with the story of how Jesus met them on the road to Emmaus. This was no ordinary story, but the recounting of a life-changing journey and encounter. For centuries, this great story has endured as one of the most popular of all Gospel accounts. It is certainly the most personal and stirring post-resurrection story ever told. For that reason, many churches still tell it every year during the Easter season.

In addition, the Emmaus story is everyone's story. It is a reflection of our lives as we walk on life's dusty road and have a personal encounter with the living Christ. It plumbs the depths of our own desire to experience nearness with the One who is wholly other. It lifts us out of the mundane and sometimes weary daily activities, showing us that God is always present and ready to touch our frustration, our misgivings, and our fears, with healing.

Let me tell you Cleopas' story in my own interpretive way. It may even be fairly close to the way it was actually told by Cleopas and his companion.

> *Greetings in the name of our living Savior. My name is Cleopas, and I want to tell you what happened to my wife and me on the Passover Sabbath. First, though, let me tell you a bit about my background. You see, I was one of those disciples who followed after Jesus, listened to His teaching, and watched His miracles. I kept saying to myself, "Surely this man has to be the Messiah. And when He overthrows the Roman government, I'm going to have a good job." Well, you can imagine how I felt on that Friday when they put Him to death. Not only was this the loss of the man I so admired, but it was also the loss of the career I had expected. My wife and I were in total despair.*
>
> *On the Sabbath, we were walking on the road to Emmaus, making our way home. Of course, the conversation went back to the events of the weekend. "Why?" we kept asking, "Why was this good man,*

*this man whom we thought to be the Messiah, put to death?"*

*It was such an incredibly burdensome question. I couldn't lift my head or straighten my shoulders if I tried. My whole body felt depressed. I was so burdened with sadness that every step of the way felt like a shuffle into nothingness. I don't know when I have ever felt so distraught, so disconnected with my surroundings, so unwilling to accept the reality of recent events.*

*After what seemed like an eternity, I glanced past my wife and noticed that there was another person walking with us. Of course, there is nothing unusual about that on the road to Emmaus. It's a highly traveled road and strangers will often meet on the road, walk together, and talk as they travel. I must admit I was a bit irritated by the stranger's presence. Too wrapped up in my own sorrow, I wanted to continue talking to my wife about our grief and disappointment.*

*Fortunately for me, this person was sensitive to the sadness in our faces, our eyes, our drooping posture — our bodies spoke louder than our words. So instead of talking about something I didn't want to talk about, he posed just the right question: "What are you talking about that makes you so sad?" he inquired, looking right at me.*

*Even though I wanted to answer his question — to talk about the death of Jesus — I felt a rush of blood to my face and was overcome with anguish once again. Frankly, I felt the stranger should have known. It seemed to me that a cloud of despair had descended upon all Jerusalem. How could anybody not know what had happened on that awful Friday? I looked up at this stranger, and in a voice that I'm sure betrayed my distress said, "We've just suffered the greatest loss of our lives. For three years we have traveled off and on with Jesus of Nazareth, a prophet who continually did wonderful things for all the people, especially the poor and needy. He seemed the favorite of God as well as man. We were sure he would deliver all of Israel from the Roman yoke. But this past weekend the chief priests and the rulers of Rome held a mock trial and condemned him and put him to death on a cross.*

*"It's been so confusing because if there was ever a person who should have been anointed King, it was Jesus. And just today we have heard rumors that his buried body has disappeared! There is even a report that some of the women from our group went to the tomb, found that it was empty, and were told by some angels that Jesus is alive. Can you imagine that? It has to be wishful thinking. After all, we saw him dead with our own eyes! We were there when he was laid in the tomb. We even helped roll a huge stone in front of the tomb."*

*The words just spilled out of my mouth, and once again I felt the sorrow and the burden of the thoughts I had been mulling over for the last few days. "It's all over. We're sick about the whole thing. So we're just going to go home and try to put our lives back together again."*

*Then the stranger looked right into my eyes and said*

14

*something I couldn't understand: "You know you are really a very forgetful person, a person whose heart works at a very slow pace. Don't you remember the teaching of the prophets? The prophets taught that the true Messiah was not someone who was to overthrow Rome and set up a political kingdom. The true Messiah, the prophets taught, had to first suffer, and then enter into the glory of the Kingdom — a kingdom that is not of this world."*

*I was amazed at his answer and, to be honest, somewhat put off. I felt this man really didn't understand what was going on; but then, as we walked he began to interpret the Scriptures from Moses and all the prophets. I heard him say things that I had never heard before; or at least if I'd heard them, they never registered with me. I still remember vividly his comments about the need for the Messiah to suffer. Maybe I remember this most because the idea was so remote from my mind. Like others, I could only think of a reigning Messiah, a great warrior who would smite our enemy Rome and set up his rule over Israel to the wild and ecstatic cheers of the whole population. But this man was talking about a suffering Messiah, a man despised and rejected, a man of sorrow. A Messiah who was oppressed and afflicted, cut off from the land of the living, a man who was crushed, and whose life was voluntarily poured out in death.*

*I didn't completely understand it. But, for some unexplainable reason, it sounded right to me. So I listened intently as this stranger went on to tell me a side of the story that literally made my heart burn* within me. "You know," he said, "the suffering of this Messiah was for you." And then he went back again to the prophet Isaiah. He told me, in the most gentle yet authoritative voice I had ever heard, "He took on your infirmity and sorrow, he was smitten and afflicted for you, he took on your transgressions, he was crushed for your iniquity. And when he was oppressed and afflicted he did not open his mouth. He went to his death, like a lamb to the slaughter."

As he was speaking, my mind went back to Friday, to the crucifixion. I had wondered even as they nailed him to the cross: Why didn't he cry out at the injustice? Why was he so silent? I remember feeling the dread of that awful silence. I wanted to scream out myself, but I was frozen in fear and amazement. There was no sound within me — I had no voice. I could scarcely feel myself breathing. At the same time, I felt like yelling, "Somebody do something! Somebody yell! Do anything that will break this awful silence!" I wanted to stamp my foot on the top of the earth and watch it disintegrate. I wanted to grab the sun and throw it smashing into little pieces all over the earth. I wanted to destroy everything around me because I felt, "This can't be. This man doesn't deserve this. He's the best thing that has ever happened to Israel. Can't you see it? Can't you see it? Can't you see it?" But I had no voice. Only this gut-wrenching feeling that everything, everything was falling apart — crumbling before my very eyes.

As we continued to walk the Emmaus road, the stranger began to tell me more. "I've told you the bad news," he said. "Now let me tell you the good news." My ears really picked up on this statement. Slowly

he began, "By his wounds," he said, "you are healed."
Those words pierced into my heart like a speeding
arrow. If ever I needed to be healed it was right then.
As he was speaking, I couldn't grasp the full impact
of that Good News, but somehow I knew he was
speaking the truth. I felt his words on the inside, and
a healing calm swept from my heart to every part of
my body. My eyes lit up, and for the first time in
days, I broke into a smile. Turning to my wife, I saw
the relief and joy in her eyes. Even though her eyes
were filled with tears, her face was radiant with a
glory that told me she too had heard, really heard,
the Good News!

I sensed this was a turning point for me, but I wasn't
sure why. Soon, though, the reason became evident.

We were not far from home. As we drew near, it was
obvious that our companion had farther to go. It was
late at night, and even though I did not know much
about this man, I felt he understood me and grasped
my despair. I also felt he knew something about the
life and death of Jesus that I didn't know. Wanting
to know more, in the fashion of good Jewish hospitality I asked, "Would you like to stay in our home?"

"Yes, thank you," he said, in a tone of voice that
communicated genuine friendship, even though we
had only walked together for a couple of hours.

We all entered the house and walked into the
kitchen. We were tired and hungry. It had been a
long, arduous journey and a wrenching emotional
experience. Being physically and emotionally
exhausted, I opened the cupboard and pulled out a

17

bottle of wine, a loaf of bread, some nuts, and dried fruit. I took the food over to the table and set it in the middle. "Ahhh," I thought to myself, "This is a better way to end the day: my wife and I and this new friend — eating together."

My new friend, however, walked over to the table and stood in my place, the place of the host. Before I had a chance to protest, I watched in amazement as this fellow traveler picked up the loaf of bread. He lifted it above his head and prayed the Jewish prayer over bread that I've prayed a thousand times: "Blessed are you, Lord our God, King of the universe, for you nourish us and the whole world with goodness, grace, kindness, and mercy. Blessed are you, Lord, for you nourish the universe." I knew these words by heart. But for some reason, the way he said these words made me feel that he understood something about this blessing that I didn't — that he had some authority I lacked. The passion and conviction in his voice as he said these words pulled at the very strings of my heart. I looked up and concentrated my attention on his hands, tightly wrapped around both ends of the loaf. I noticed there was something different about his hands, but I wasn't sure what it was. They had the appearance of having been mauled, but they were beautiful, sturdy, strong hands that said something about this man's character.

Suddenly his hands went into action. He broke the bread, dividing it into two. The break was gentle, but what I saw in my mind's eye was violent. The bread was being torn asunder. It was as though the bread was assaulted and abused, broken in violence, *torn viciously, and crushed unmercifully. Another thought ran through my head. This stranger's interpretation of Isaiah 53 brought the crucifixion events to mind. Suddenly the bread was no longer bread; it was the body of Jesus. The memory of his horribly excruciating death returned vividly. I heard the hammering of the nails and the taunts of derision, saw the plunge of the sword. But most of all, I was aware of the deafening silence of Jesus. And then the words of the stranger welled up inside me, and I heard a voice say, "By his wounds you are healed."*

*My eyes dropped to the uplifted face of the traveller. His face was lit like the sun, and I saw angels all around. They were singing, "Worthy is the lamb that was slain to receive power and wealth and wisdom and honor and glory and blessing." In that instant I knew our guest was no ordinary man. This stranger in our midst was the resurrected Jesus. An involuntary voice came rushing out of my inner being, and I heard myself cry, "It's Jesus! He's alive again!" My knees gave way and I literally slumped to the floor. I looked up to see Jesus again, but he was gone — vanished from my sight.*

*A flood of emotions pulsated through my body. I felt as though I had been invaded by light, as though I had just been born from my mother's womb but with a full consciousness of my surroundings. Nothing looked the same anymore. All of life was transformed, and the words Jesus had spoken on the road were swirling around in my head. Once again the Good News came to the surface: "By his wounds, you are healed."*

*"Yes!" I shouted, "Yes, yes! I see it! Why was I so slow to understand? His kingdom is not the politics of Caesar; His kingdom is not an earthly reign. His kingdom, His rule, is right here in my heart. He rules me and all others who put their trust in Him. He is Lord!" Instinctively, my wife and I both knelt. Looking up into the eternal presence of the resurrected Christ, we worshiped and adored him, crying, "You are Lord! Indeed you are Lord and we bow before you."*

*We stood once again and embraced in the joy of our comprehension. My wife looked up into my eyes then and spoke my name. "Cleopas," she said, "we have to return to Jerusalem and tell the disciples that we've seen Jesus, the resurrected Jesus!"*

*I knew in my heart that she was right, but I was so tired after our journey and the emotional meeting that my first thought was, "It's seven long miles. I'm tired; it's too late; we won't get there until early in the morning." Then I heard the gentle but insistent urging of my wife, "Come, Cleopas. Let's go right now."*

*Frankly, I don't remember the details of our return trip; but I know sometimes we walked, sometimes we ran with sudden energy. The words of my conversation with Jesus kept coming to mind: "By his wounds you are healed." They were taking root in my soul. I could feel the healing process in my own body and mind, and so could my wife.*

*This trip went fast, much faster than I expected. We arrived in Jerusalem just as the sun was coming up, and I heard a rooster welcoming the day. "How appropriate!" I thought to myself. "It's a new day, and we can tell the disciples that it's a new beginning for us all." And so we found them gathered in a second-story room for prayer.*

*Needless to say, although we were exhausted, we were so full of excitement that we dashed hurriedly up the steps, burst through the door, and cried, "The Lord is risen! He is risen indeed, for we knew him in the breaking of the bread!"*

*The eyes of the disciples grew wide with astonishment. As one man they rose and hurried to our side, begging, "Tell us! Tell us what you have seen." They too had heard rumors of Jesus' resurrection, but had not seen or met anyone with firsthand information. So we told them our story. Just as we were describing how we had recognized Jesus in the breaking of the bread, all of a sudden there he was: Jesus — he just appeared among us, held out his hands in a gesture of welcome and said, "Peace be with you."*

*I think we were all frightened. I know I was, but mostly we were just absolutely awestruck. We fell at his feet, babbling questions in a jumble of chaotic words. "Jesus, what's going on? Tell us the meaning of all this."*

*In the middle of all the frenzy, I heard Jesus ask, "Do you have any food?" Into my mind came the revelation in the breaking of the bread. My heart pounding, I could sense what was to come. We ate together and once again I listened, enraptured by the words of Jesus healing my heart and bringing life to my soul.*

21

*Well, as you know, I'm a member of the church of Jerusalem. Every time we gather to worship, we break bread; and Jesus — the resurrected Jesus — shows up to touch us, to heal us, and once again to make us whole.*

\* \* \* \* \* \*

The story recounted by Cleopas has everything to do with our experience of the presence of God. It is actually the story of an incredible worship experience for Cleopas and his wife because it changed their lives forever. The Emmaus story is also a pattern for *our* experience of God's presence. Worship scholars look to this passage as a key that unlocks the door to early Christian worship in which God's presence was manifest.

Let's reflect now on a few of the crucial elements of this story: Cleopas and his companion were on a journey. It was on that journey that they met the resurrected Christ, even though they did not yet recognize him. It was on the journey that Jesus began to open the Scripture to them. He explained and revealed the Scriptures in such a way that their hearts began to burn with insight and revelation. Next they arrived in Emmaus and offered Jesus the hospitality of their home because he had become their traveling companion. It was in the breaking of the bread that the most astonishing thing happened. In the breaking of the bread they recognized Jesus, the resurrected Christ, who was present with them at the table. Finally, even though Jesus disappeared from their midst, they were overwhelmed with joy and the desire to tell others. Immediately they set out on that long, seven-mile hike back to Jerusalem to tell the other disciples they had seen and experienced the presence of the resurrected Jesus.

Here then is the pattern of our personal and public worship, the means by which we journey into the presence of God.

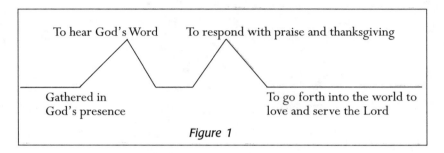

Figure 1

Stage one: Our journey into God's presence begins *when we are on the way.*

Stage two: Our Journey into God's presence continues as *we hear the Word of God in our heart.*

Stage three: The climactic point of our journey occurs *at the Table where Jesus' presence is experienced in a highly intensive way.*

Stage Four: Our journey continues as *we go forth joyfully telling others and living only to serve the resurrected Christ.*

The Emmaus journey is our journey into His presence. Worship, both personal and public is a journey – my journey, your journey – into the very presence of God.

## Thinking It Over

1) Consider all the things you do to get ready for a journey. List them or talk about them.
2) Remember and tell a favorite story of how God showed Himself strong on your behalf.

3) Choose any story in the New Testament and tell it as you think it may have been told by one of the characters in the story.

# tage One of the Journey: On the Road

*Jesus himself came up and walked along with them (Luke 24:15).*

As we explore our journey into His presence, a close look at Cleopas' experience will guide our way. See him again — immensely disappointed in the death of Jesus. All his hopes and dreams were shattered, and we observe his sad eyes, drooping mouth, head hung low, body rounded by the weight of his fears. But Cleopas did one thing right: He got on the road.

## Our Personal Journey

On our own *Road to Emmaus*, we need to identify our dislocations just as Cleopas did. We live in a complicated and fast-moving world; yet even in the busyness of our lives, our bodies and souls, too, are rounded by the weight of our burdens. We, like Cleopas, need hope in the midst of the turmoil that surrounds us; and God — our burden bearer — is ready and waiting to give us that hope. So we should take all of our problems *on the road* and not leave them behind.

For us, getting on the road means that we must make an honest evaluation of where we are. Admitting our problems, our failures, our distractions, our sins, and our dislocation means that we have made the first step that will put us on the road leading right into the presence of God. In God's presence our lives will be transformed, and we will be given a way to deal with the issues that seem to overwhelm us.

25

To fully understand what we are about to do, there is another dimension of Cleopas that needs to be explored: his disposition.

If we were to peel away all the distractions that were dominating the life of Cleopas, I think we would find, underneath it all, a disposition of openness. He had certainly not closed the door to the presence of God, but he misunderstood it. Like others, he wanted a political Messiah. But when he learned he was misinformed, he did not cling to his misunderstanding. He allowed himself to be transformed because he was open and ready. Maybe the door wasn't wide open, but it wasn't shut and locked. There was a crack there, ready to burst open. When we are on the road, we have to expect that anything can happen. We need to keep the door of our hearts open, even if it's only a little teeny crack. God can break through that door and transform us by His presence.

Let's also keep in mind that Cleopas was not on the road alone. His companion journeyed with him, but they were alone in their interpretation of events; they were unaware that Jesus was walking the road with them. When we begin the journey into personal or public worship, we also are never alone. God is always present, traveling with us on the road; and so is the great angelic host – the cherubim, the seraphim, angels, and archangels – and those who have gone before us. We are, as the writer of Hebrews tells us, "surrounded by such a great cloud of witnesses" (Hebrews 12:1).

On the road to worship, we approach the invisible God. We don't know this God who dwells in inaccessible light, this God who is incomprehensible, this God who is wholly other, until we see the shining face of God in Jesus Christ. And this surprise, which never grows old, happens again and again. It happened for Cleopas; it can happen for us.

It happens for us, not only in our private worship, but also in the public worship of the church. Here we are on the road to the presence of God. Let's look at how we get on the road in corporate worship.

## Our Corporate Journey into the Presence

Coming together to worship corporately is not unlike the experience of Cleopas. First, we need to get on the road.

For example, not long ago I visited a mega-church I had been hearing about quite a bit. As my companion and I drew closer to the church, we soon became part of the jam of hundreds of cars all streaming to the church. My immediate response was, "The *Procession* has begun, and we are part of it." The journey begins at home, and it continues as people stream to the place of worship and into God's presence.

The first act of public worship initiated by God is the calling to gather. Cleopas didn't know it, but he was called to get on the road to worship. And so are we. For us, the gathering may begin on Saturday night as we protect our time and refrain from engagements that exhaust us and prevent our full involvement in worship. We may select clothes for ourselves and the children to wear. We set our alarms; we get up. We eat. We get dressed. We drive to church. We enter God's house. We assemble in God's presence. All these acts are acts of Gathering which will culminate eventually in an intense encounter with God.

## The Biblical Foundation

The Biblical idea of gathering, or "getting together on the road," is expressed in the word *assembly*. It has a rich and powerful meaning in the history of Biblical worship because it refers to the specific act of coming together before the Lord.

27

This idea of assembly is already present in Luke 24. First, in verses 1-12, the women assembled at the tomb; the story of Cleopas illustrates this act of coming together.

We find its earliest use in the gathering of Israel at the foot of Mt. Sinai, where Israel covenanted with God to love Him, to serve Him, and to worship Him (Exodus 24:1-8). From that time forward Israel was known as the *Qahal*, literally "to-call-together community." God's call was on Israel; they were His people and He summoned them again and again to assemble — to get on the road and gather in His presence. Israel assembled at the Tabernacle; assembled at David's Tent; assembled at the Temple; and, in the Dispersion, they assembled around the Torah. This assembling has continued throughout history. It goes on today wherever we gather to worship; and at the end of history, there will be a worldwide gathering of people who will stream to the mountain of worship. Isaiah testifies:

> In the last days the mountain of the Lord's temple
> will be established as chief among the mountains;
> it will be raised above the hills, and all nations will
> stream to it.  Many peoples will come and say,
> "Come, let us go up to the mountain of the Lord,
> to the house of the God of Jacob. He will teach us
> his ways, so that we may walk in his paths"
> (Isaiah 2:2-3).

Isaiah gives us a glorious vision of people all over the world streaming to the mountain of God. They come in droves. Millions and millions of people come to assemble at the mountain where God is present, so that they may be taught His ways and walk in His paths. In this context every one of us, therefore, is a Cleopas.

This same theme of assembly, of gathering together to be in

28

God's presence, is continued in the New Testament. The very word *Church (ecclesia)* means "those who are called out." In the New Testament, God has called from all the peoples of the earth a new community – the Church – to assemble at Mt. Calvary and to worship Him. Consequently, the writer of Hebrews admonishes, "Let us not give up meeting together [assembling]…but let us encourage one another – and all the more as you see the Day approaching" (Hebrews 10:25). When Paul addresses the church at Corinth he says, "I hear that when you come together as a church …" (I Corinthians 11:18). It is even more meaningful when we discover that the word Paul uses for *come together* is *synaxis,* a special word which means *to gather the church in the presence of God.* (See Figure 2)

## A Biblical Description of Gathering

Probably the most dramatic example of the Gathering recorded in Scripture is described by the writer of II Chronicles on the day when the ark was brought into the Temple:

> All the Levites who were musicians – Asaph, Heman, Jeduthun and their sons and relatives – stood on the east side of the altar, dressed in fine linen and playing cymbals, harps and lyres. They were accompanied by 120 priests sounding trumpets. The trumpeters and singers joined in unison, as with one voice, to give praise and thanks to the Lord. Accompanied by trumpets, cymbals and other instruments, they raised their voices in praise to the Lord and sang: "He is good; his love endures forever." Then the temple of the Lord was filled with a cloud, and the priests could not perform their service because of the cloud, *for the glory of the Lord filled the temple of God* (II Chronicles 5:12-14, emphasis mine).

29

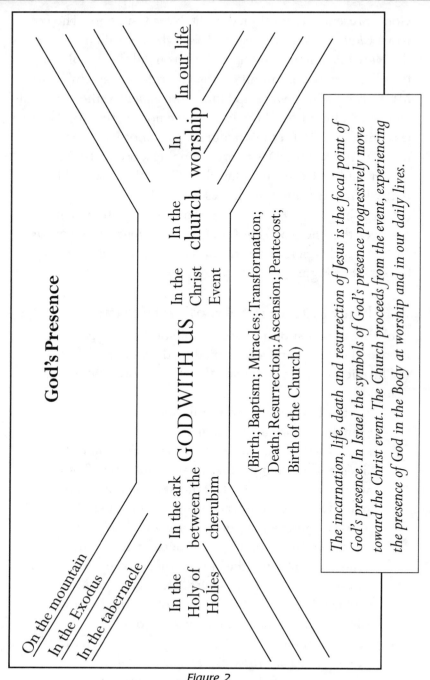

**God's Presence**

On the mountain
In the Exodus
In the tabernacle

In the Holy of Holies

In the ark between the cherubim

GOD WITH US

In the Christ Event

(Birth; Baptism; Miracles; Transformation; Death; Resurrection; Ascension; Pentecost; Birth of the Church)

In the church

worship

In our life

*The incarnation, life, death and resurrection of Jesus is the focal point of God's presence. In Israel the symbols of God's presence progressively move toward the Christ event. The Church proceeds from the event, experiencing the presence of God in the Body at worship and in our daily lives.*

*Figure 2*

30

There is no question that the bringing of the ark to the Temple and the gathering of the people to enter into God's presence was a momentous occasion. There was no missing the moment here! All the stops were pulled out, and the gathering was accompanied by pomp, ceremony, processions, banners, the sounds of many instruments and voices in praise of God. What they experienced, of course, was what we all want to experience – the revelation of God's presence, a presence so intense that their words and feeble attempts to worship were silenced in their awe.

## The Gathering Today

The Biblical example of the gathering at the Temple raises this question: What function does the gathering accomplish in worship? The gathering for worship is much more than just a group of people being brought together out of their own initiative. It is a calling, a calling from God to assemble in His presence to worship Him and to be formed by Him as His special community on earth – the called-out ones. Therefore, a gathering will bring us into the presence of God and make us ready to hear the Word of the Lord. Certainly this is what happened to Cleopas.

## Confusion Regarding the Gathering

Many churches are unaware of the Biblical significance and the purpose of the gathering. For example, it is popular today to follow a twofold pattern of worship: singing and teaching. Some churches add a third aspect: ministry.

In these churches, the thirty minutes of singing is called "The Worship Time." In this line of thinking, however, there is a disassociation of the sermon, intercessory prayer, communion, and other acts of worship from *worship*. We act as though worship is expressed only or primarily in song.

31

This attitude is demonstrated when we say to the minister of music, "The worship was great today!" Then, almost as an afterthought, we say to the pastor, "Your sermon wasn't too bad either." (As if the sermon was not worship!)

This perception of worship as the time of singing is fairly widespread in some circles. For example, I discussed this issue with a worship leader whose comment to me was, "Bob, face it. Music is the new sacrament." By using the word *sacrament*, he meant "the means by which God becomes present to us." Then he said, "Until the Reformation the chief sacrament was the Eucharist. The reformers replaced the Eucharist with the sacrament of the Word. Today the primary encounter with God occurs in our music."

Certainly, no one will argue against music being very important in worship. The Bible is filled with examples of using music in worship. Music helps us to express the emotional content of our worship. For this reason music may be the wheels that symbolize and express the gathering. And there is nothing wrong about a thirty-minute sung gathering. We only need to recognize that it is not the *whole* of worship. It could instead be considered the first act of worship: the coming together of God's people to be a worshiping community.

An analogy for the Gathering is to liken it to the foyer of the home where we exchange greetings and say words or do actions such as handshaking or hugging to express our relationship. The gathering in the foyer is the appropriate place for our greetings and for the relational reconnections we make there. *But we don't expect to stay there.* We go on to a deeper interaction in the living room. So it is in God's house. In the Gathering we reconnect with God and then proceed into *God's* living room to learn His ways so we can walk in His paths.

## The Gathering As the Journey of Our Coming into the Presence of God

The Gathering is not a program. It is not a willy-nilly collection of acts of worship done without any connection and without any process of movement. Instead, the Gathering puts us on the road where we hear the voice of God, we respond with praise and thanksgiving, and we go forth to love and serve the Lord.

I want to illustrate the process and meaning of the Gathering by providing you with two examples to consider:
  • the Gathering in traditional worship
  • the Gathering in contemporary worship

## The Gathering in Traditional Worship

My example of traditional worship comes from an Episcopal church service, where the service is ordered by the *Book of Common Prayer*.

As I entered the church, I quietly knelt and began to pray with others. Following this time of individual preparatory prayer, the prelude was played, and then a great and marvelous procession of minister and choir joyously marched to the altar area. (Episcopalian processions are really magnificent!) We sang a marvelous hymn with the procession. (Although some traditional churches have sung *choruses* in the Gathering, this rarely seems to work well. A hymn with weight and substance is required to accompany the movement of the procession.)

33

Following the procession I heard the *call to worship*. (Keep in mind that this is God's call to assemble.) In the *Book of Common Prayer*, this call begins, *"Blessed be God: Father, Son and Holy Spirit."* Right away the Trinitarian nature of worship has been expressed. (We come to *praise* the Father, *thank* the Son and *invoke* the presence of the Holy Spirit among us.)

We all responded, *"And blessed be His Kingdom now and forever. Amen."* These words are a joyous acclamation. They are not simply intellectual. They go deeper. They express our relationship to God. We are His people, His Kingdom, the people in whom He dwells.

Then, the call to worship was followed by an *invocation*. An invocation is a calling upon God to be present to the community. I heard this historic and magnificent prayer for God's presence in a new way:

> *Almighty God to whom all hearts are open, all*
> *desires known, and from whom no secrets are hid,*
> *cleanse the thoughts of our hearts by the inspiration*
> *of Your Holy Spirit that we may perfectly love You*
> *and worthily magnify Your Holy name through Jesus*
> *Christ, Our Lord. Amen.*

This prayer is very brief, and it invokes the presence of God to clean us up so that what we offer to God will be a pure act of worship. I felt it to be a most fitting request as we moved into the presence of God.

In this prayer we pray from our hearts: *"God come; connect with us. Be present to us!"* That plea is the invocation. Thus we have shared a narrative progression, rich with symbolic meaning, and not mere disjointed acts of worship.

The procession, the call to worship, the invocation have brought us into the presence of God. It is then and only then that we break forth into praise! What else? Here we are in the presence of God Almighty! The only appropriate response is to praise God, to lift our hearts and voices in response to God's mighty otherness and incomprehensible deity. The great hymn that is sung in many traditional churches, at this point, is the *Gloria in Excelsis Deo*. I love this hymn because we enthrone the Father, we enthrone the Son, we enthrone the Holy Spirit. It is one of the most joyful and moving hymns of the church. Here are the words of that great hymn — one of the oldest and most treasured of the church:

> *Glory to God in the highest,*
> *and peace to His people on earth.*
>
> *Lord God, heavenly King,*
> *almighty God and Father,*
> *we worship You, we give You thanks,*
> *we praise You for your glory.*
>
> *Lord Jesus Christ, only Son of the Father,*
> *Lord God, Lamb of God,*
> *You take away the sins of the world:*
> *have mercy on us,*
> *You are seated at the right hand of the Father —*
> *receive our prayer.*
>
> *For You alone are the Holy one,*
> *You alone are the Lord,*
> *You alone are the most high,*
> *Jesus Christ*
> *with the Holy Spirit in the glory of God the Father.*
> *Amen.*

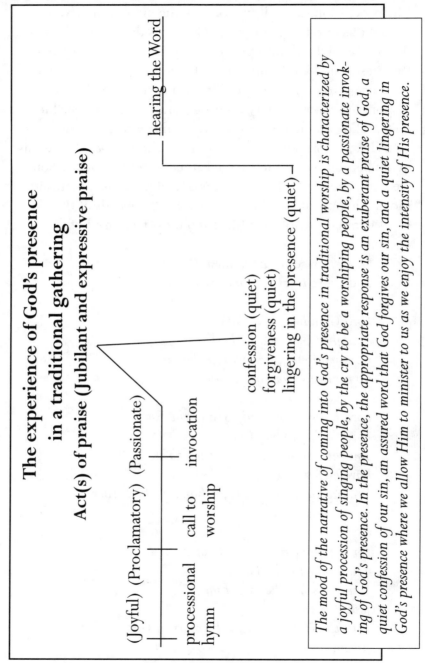

**The experience of God's presence in a traditional gathering**

**Act(s) of praise (Jubilant and expressive praise)**

hearing the Word

confession (quiet)
forgiveness (quiet)
lingering in the presence (quiet)

(Joyful) (Proclamatory) (Passionate)

processional
hymn

call to
worship

invocation

*The mood of the narrative of coming into God's presence in traditional worship is characterized by a joyful procession of singing people, by the cry to be a worshiping people, by a passionate invoking of God's presence. In the presence, the appropriate response is an exuberant praise of God, a quiet confession of our sin, an assured word that God forgives our sin, and a quiet lingering in God's presence where we allow Him to minister to us as we enjoy the intensity of His presence.*

*Figure 3*

Singing the *Gloria in Excelsis Deo* is an experience of the transcendence, the otherness of God like that recounted in the beginning of Isaiah, chapter 6:

> ...I saw the Lord seated on a throne, high and exalted, and the train of his robe filled the temple... "Woe to me!" I cried. "I am ruined. For I am a man of unclean lips, and I live among a people of unclean lips, and my eyes have seen the King, the Lord Almighty."

When we have engaged in the Isaiah experience of the God who is Beyond, a God who is incomprehensible, we recognize our sinful condition and like Isaiah cry, "*Woe to me! ... For I am a man of unclean lips.*" I was ready for that confession. I wanted to cry out:

> *Lord have mercy.*
> *Christ have mercy.*
> *Lord have mercy.*

After worship, I took some time to reflect on the traditional gathering. What was happening? I saw that the purpose of these actions of worship were to order and organize our experience of coming into the presence of God. God's special community was now formed. We had centered and focused on God. We were ready to hear God speak (see Figure 3). Before we look at *how* God speaks, let's look at another Gathering narrative, the one that takes place in today's contemporary church.

## The Gathering in Contemporary Worship

The traditional church and the contemporary church actually follow a similar journey but with a very different style. The contemporary church models itself after the Tabernacle journey of the Old Testament.

This music-driven Gathering takes about thirty minutes. For a moment imagine yourself in Israel. God's people are coming to the gates to worship the Lord. All are singing; some are bringing banners, some are playing timbrels, and others are dancing as they sing. It's kind of noisy. The journey takes us into the outer court, then the inner court, and finally into the very throne room of God, the Holy of Holies.

Many contemporary churches follow this model. They begin at the gates with a familiar song, like Kirk Dearman's "We Bring the Sacrifice of Praise into the House of the Lord." This joyous chorus brings the worshipers closer to the presence of God. From the gates, the community progresses symbolically into the outer court; the music at this point reflects the mood of coming to worship with songs like "As We Gather" by Mike Fay and Tom Loomes. The next transition is into the Inner Court. Here the songs are more quiet and intense, and they are about God's nature, such as "Great Is the Lord" by Michael W. Smith and Deborah D. Smith. Finally, the congregation is brought into the Holy of Holies. In many churches the people will sing "Create in Me a Clean Heart, O God" (composer unknown) at this point. It's good to end with relational songs to God such as Laurie Klein's "I Love You Lord."

An example may be helpful to those who are less familiar with contemporary-style renewal worship services:

> During a trip to Anaheim, California, I decided to visit the Vineyard Church, which at that time was led by the late John Wimber. I had never been to a Vineyard service before and was curious about their style of worship. It was a big church. At that particular time they had a building that appeared like

38

*an airplane hanger, but with seating for between
4,000 and 6,000 people. There was a huge plat-
form up front with all the symbols of contemporary
worship: three microphones for the worship leaders, a
keyboard instrument (in this case a synthesizer)
along with drums and a guitar. Eddie Espinosa led
worship with the guitar and gathered us into the
presence of God. We sang for thirty minutes, starting
with high praise, during which people were moving
their bodies and raising their hands in the air. The
singing became gradually more and more quiet.
When we reached that meditative state of relationship in the Holy of Holies, I noticed that there were
about a dozen people who left their seats. They
approached the altar and lay prostrate on the floor
as the community continued to sing.*

This is the place where we want to be in worship. We want to
bow down and humble ourselves before the Almighty. In the
Old and New Testament, when people worshiped they bowed
down. Overcome by the awareness of the holiness of God's
presence, people fell on their faces.

Now let's go back and review the journey into God's
presence in the contemporary style. Let's agree that this is
not our "worship time" exclusively, but the process by which
we are assembled (in the Biblical sense) in the presence of
God and made ready to hear the Word of God. Everything
the contemporary church does in the Gathering it can
continue to do. Their sung narrative has within it the power to
order and organize the spirit into a position of quiet
reverence, an openness and vulnerability to God that will
continue throughout the other acts of worship. In the
Gathering we enter the Presence where we remain for the

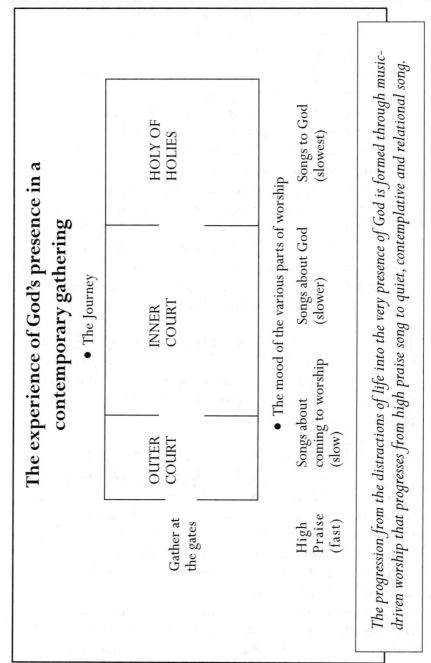

## The experience of God's presence in a contemporary gathering

● The Journey

| OUTER COURT | INNER COURT | HOLY OF HOLIES |
|---|---|---|

● The mood of the various parts of worship

| Gather at the gates | Songs about coming to worship (slow) | Songs about God (slower) | Songs to God (slowest) |
|---|---|---|---|
| High Praise (fast) | | | |

*The progression from the distractions of life into the very presence of God is formed through music-driven worship that progresses from high praise song to quiet, contemplative and relational song.*

*Figure 4*

duration of our time together with God. We understand that as with Cleopas, God is walking the journey with us in our corporate worship. (See Figure 4.)

## Bringing Stage One into Focus

The journey Cleopas took toward the presence of God is analogous to the journey we take in both private and public worship. Worship has to start someplace, and it always starts on the road. Whatever burdens or issues trouble our lives and bring distress to us should never be left behind. We always bring them with us in personal and corporate worship.

The message for all of us is that we need to recover the wonder of coming into the presence of God. In private worship, we need to know that nothing is hidden from God. We can't hide any of our dislocations, so we need to come before God like Cleopas in radical honesty about what we are thinking. We need to be open to the presence of God. In public worship we are free to use pomp and ceremony, to revel in the act of coming into God's presence, to use our many musicians, to restore processions with banners and dance, and to come into God's presence with great joy and a spirit of celebration.

In this calling of public worship we are free to abandon ourselves to Him. There is no missing of the moment when it is vested with such glory. Let's allow the sounds, the traveling of the procession, the visual imagery of banners and people to ignite our spiritual imaginations! Let's allow ourselves to feel the very presence of Almighty God.

Then let's allow ourselves to be aware of the assembled body. I am not talking about a mere intellectual awareness, but a realization of I Corinthians 12 that this is the Body of Christ on earth, a body joined with the head in a mystical union accomplished by the presence of God. Look around you and see the hands and feet, the voices, the eyes, the ears of the body. Take a moment to reflect on the parts of the body distinguished by the gifts they bring to the assembly. Let yourself connect with the whole body so you can find your place in the worship and service of God.

Take time to *center*. Lift all the distractions of your life to God. Allow yourself to become lost in wonder and praise. Stay there for awhile. In some churches this is the moment for lingering in the presence of God. Personal prayer uttered silently or in a whisper is appropriate. Quiet singing in the spirit expresses the depth of relationship. A time of silence before God may solidify the experience of being in His presence.

After this, you are ready for the second *stage* of the journey — hearing from God through the Word.

## How Far Have We Come?

We've traveled quite a distance already; and, in the words of the panting child who needed a rest, "It's time to look at the view!" What have we realized so far?

- We don't travel the road alone — God is with us, as are a host of angels
- We identify our dislocations and take them with us for His transforming power
- We gather corporately to worship as well
- We find Biblical patterns for our gathering in His presence
- We are called by Him to gather in order to be formed into His community on earth
- We respond with praise as we are reconnected to the God who is wholly other

# Thinking It Over

1) Using the image of "On the Road," describe where you are right now in your life.

2) What do you think Cleopas or his wife would say to you about your place "On the Road"?

3) Describe the *Gathering* time in the public worship of your church. What would you do to improve it?

# tage Two of the Journey: The Burning Heart

*Beginning with Moses and all the Prophets, he explained to them what was said in all the Scriptures concerning himself (Luke 24:27).*

My dad was the kind of person who spent an enormous amount of time with the Word. One of my earliest recollections of my father, a pastor, is of him sitting in an old stuffed chair that he had put by the furnace in the basement.

> *He frequently sat there with an open Bible in his hand, reading, thinking and praying. One day, when I was about ten, I saw my dad wrapping his Bible in a newspaper. Somewhat surprised and puzzled by this, I cried, "Dad, what are you doing?"*

> *"I'm going to bury my Bible," he said. "I've worn it out and I bought a new one. You just don't throw the Bible in the trash, you know. It's the Word of God."*

> *I walked with my dad through the back yard to a stream at the edge of the woods. I watched as he dug a hole, reverently laid the Bible to rest, covered it with dirt, gave it a pat of the hand, and offered a prayer of thanks for the Word.*

My dad's attitude toward the Scripture reminds me of an incident that happened a few years ago. I had met another university professor who was vacationing at the same place I was. He was a deeply devoted Christian, a member of a house church. He had this to say to me: "You know, Bob, I want nothing more than the Word of God to take up residence within me and shape me into Christ-likeness."

My dad and my friend had exactly the right idea. Through the Word, which we prayerfully read and hear, God's presence takes up residence within us.

## Our Personal Journey into the Presence through the Word

The image of Cleopas on the road hearing the Word of God expounded and applied to his own personal hurts is a beautiful picture of how God touches us with His presence through the Word.

The only Scripture Cleopas knew was the Old Testament. He, like others in Israel, had misinterpreted the messianic hope of the Old Testament. They had expected the Messiah would be like Moses or David – a great leader who would overthrow an oppressive government.

In this story we have a direct statement of what Jesus had to say: "And beginning with Moses and all the Prophets, he explained to them what was said in all the Scriptures concerning himself" (Luke 24:27). This is why in my telling of the story, I concentrated on the Christian interpretation of Isaiah 53. Much of the early Christian literature focuses on the sacrifice of Christ on the cross. John cries out to all, "Look, the Lamb of God who takes away the sin of the world" (John 1:29). If Jesus expounded the entire Old Testament, He must have said something to Cleopas that touched on the result of His sacrifice as well. Perhaps He also said, "Cleopas, I want you to understand what's happening here. As a result of my death, the prince of this world will be cast out. This is why I can say that by My wounds you are healed." (See John 12:31 and Isaiah 53:5.)

We don't know for certain the exact words Jesus said to Cleopas, but I can't help thinking He may have told Cleopas (and later the disciples gathered in the upper room) the consequence of His suffering and death. Maybe He said that by dying He had trampled down death. By His death, "the prince of this world now stands condemned" (John 16:11) and the prince of this world "has no hold on [Him]" (John 14:30b).

The death of Christ was not only a sacrifice for the sins of the world; His sacrifice also resulted in the downfall of the powers of evil. Jesus bound the powers of evil (Matthew 12), He dethroned the powers of evil (Colossians 2:15), and at the end of history He will completely destroy the powers of evil (Revelation 20-22). For this reason we have power over evil in Jesus' name.

Let me give you a personal example of experiencing the power of God over evil.

> One night the phone rang about 1:00 a.m. On the other end of the phone, a distraught mother of a student sobbed into the phone, "Please come right away; my daughter needs you."
>
> I arrived at the home, and was immediately taken upstairs where the daughter was lying on her bed — disheveled, disoriented, and exhausted. But she had

*enough strength to say, "Go to Jim; go to Jim." Jim was her boyfriend, and he was in a nearby small room, lying on the couch. I entered the room, took one look at Jim, and realized I was dealing with a supernatural power that was strangling the life out of Jim.*

*My seminary training had not even posed this problem, let alone provided me with a way of dealing with it. But I quickly got "on the road" and called out to God: "God, this is too big and complex for me. Help!" I remembered the New Testament accounts of demon possession, so God brought to my mind the first step — identify the power. I leaned over Jim, and I cried out in a shaky but insistent voice, "Who are you?" Almost instantly a voice came out of Jim's mouth. His lips and his tongue were frozen, but an eerie voice emerged from him. "Legion," it answered. I was smart enough to know that "Legion" means "many," and I was scared.*

*"Legion," I said, "I've come here to cast you back into hell where you belong. You don't belong in Jim."*

*Then Legion spoke again: "But Jim will be lonely."*

*"No, he won't," I said firmly. "The Holy Spirit will fill his life."*

*Then I quickly launched into the reason why the Spirit would fill Jim's life. "Jesus died for Jim," I said. "Jesus paid the price."*

*And then in one of the most terrifying tones I have*

*ever heard, Legion wailed, "Why not for me? Why not for me? Why not for me?!"*

*At first I was taken aback. "Wow!" I thought, "That's a deep theological question." Then I realized it was Legion's detour. He wanted to get me side-tracked to keep me from dealing with the real issue. Instantly, God gave me these words, "Look, Legion, I didn't come here to discuss theology with you. I came here to send you back to hell by the power of the crucified and risen Jesus."*

*I placed my hands firmly around Jim's head and for the next several hours continually said, "Legion, I cast you out by the power of the blood of Jesus Christ."*

*Early that morning, through continued prayer and application of the Word, Jim was dramatically and miraculously delivered.*

What happened? "By His wounds we are healed." Christ has already won a great victory over the powers of evil, a victory that will never by reversed. This is a victory we can claim in our own lives and in our ministry with others.

Jim was healed and so was his girlfriend. Now, together as man and wife, they serve the Lord in a local church.

The Word of the Lord delivers us from whatever seeks to destroy our lives. Cleopas had been stopped in his tracks. Full of despair, loneliness, and maybe even some guilt, he stepped on the road; and Jesus the deliverer was there. His words to Cleopas began to birth new life into a distraught human being.

What's important for us in our personal encounter with the presence of God in the Word is that the life-giving words of Jesus must be immediately embraced, as they were by Cleopas. The affirmation of the words of Jesus as truth resulted in the burning heart. The internal conviction of Cleopas literally had a physical component.

We see an interesting development in the story at this point. We can actually feel a change taking place in Cleopas. We see him move from the despair he had taken on the road to new hope. He became a man with a new direction in his life as a result of the life-giving Word taking up residence and bursting forth into new life in him.

What this says to us about our personal worship is that we need to allow the life-giving Word of God to take up residence within us and shape us into Christ-likeness. We literally house the Word of God which lives in us. In this way God's presence is always among us. It becomes to us the stuff out of which we live life.

I'm going to give you a personal example of "housing" the Word. Our goal is to let the Word of God reside within. But for all of us, letting the Word of God dwell within is usually a struggle:

> *My earliest and most memorable experience of the Word taking up residence within me occurred when I was nine years old. We lived next to a small farm, and behind that farm and behind our home were numerous blackberry bushes. I loved to pick the blackberries so I could eat them on cold cereal, or eat them with milk and sugar, or in a blackberry pie — if I could talk my mother into making one. That's why*

*I would invariably choose a large pail to take with me, and my goal was always to fill it to the brim.*

*One day, as I was picking the blackberries, I ended up in the farmer's patch. The farmer saw me, ran out of his house, and yelled, "Hey kid, get off my property! Those are my blackberries, not yours. Don't ever let me catch you on my property again!" Frankly, I felt the farmer had over-reacted. He made me feel like a thief; and as I strode home, I was angry — very angry.*

*I walked into my house, found my father, and angrily told him how I was accosted by this farmer. My father stood and grabbed my hand. "Come on, Robert. We're going to go next door and talk to the farmer."*

*I thought to myself, "Yes! My dad will give him a piece of his mind and yell at that farmer like the farmer yelled at me. I want to see this."*

*When we knocked, the farmer came to the door with a scowl on his face. My dad reached over and took the handle of my bucket which was overflowing with succulent, ripe blackberries. He opened the screen door and moved the bucket close to the farmer. In a quiet voice Dad said, "I'm really sorry my son was picking your blackberries. Here, please take these blackberries, and I promise it will never happen again."*

*I was flabbergasted. That farmer was an old crab. He just wanted to yell at me and make me feel bad. I wanted a tooth for a tooth. He yelled at me; we should yell at him. Isn't that the way it works? Here was my dad, doing the opposite of what I thought should be done.*

*It was obvious that the farmer was stunned by my father's quiet words and gestures. His face, no longer scowling, lit up and became relaxed. Then he said, "Look, I'm really sorry I yelled at your boy. We never pick those blackberries. Keep them. And furthermore, I give you permission to pick all the blackberries you want from our back yard."*

*My father reached out his hand to the farmer, gave his hand a strong shake, smiled, and said, "Thank you. You're a good neighbor."*

*Then my father reached down to me, took my hand and said, "Let's go home." When we were about half way between the two homes, my father looked at me and said, "Robert, you can learn a good lesson from this incident." I looked up at him as he continued, "A gentle answer turns away wrath, but a harsh word stirs up anger" (Proverbs 15:1). In that moment my heart housed those words as truth. In fact, my heart was burning with the presence of God's Word. I vowed then and there to live by those words.*

Here, of course, is the point. The presence of God takes up residence inside us when we choose to house the Word of God and to let his Word shape the way we live. The psalmist understood this when he wrote, "Your word is a lamp to my feet and a light for my path" (Psalm 119:105). Cleopas illustrated this choice when he invited Jesus into his house.

Today, the presence of God is with us through God's Word. We need to read and study the Word to "house" the overarching Christian story that reaches from creation to the consummation of history. In this most powerful of stories, meaning is given to life and hope is born.

We also need to deliberately take our personal problems to the Word in search of a word that we can "house" and follow. Whatever our problem may be – there is a word for us within the Word. And when that Word abides with us and shapes our life, we are living in the presence of God who is always present through His Word. This is what it means to have a personal relationship with God.

Let's turn now to the place of the Word in our public worship.

## The Presence of God through the Word in Public Worship

The story of Cleopas gives us a strong clue concerning what should happen in the service of the Word in public worship: "And beginning with Moses and all the Prophets, he explained to them what was said in all the Scriptures concerning himself" (Luke 24:27). What lies at the heart of public worship is the *recitation of God's mighty deeds of salvation.*

### The Biblical Foundation

In the earliest description of worship, found in Acts 2:42, Luke informs us that the early Christians gathered around the "Apostles' teaching." This content of the service of the Word is the Apostolic tradition which was first preached and then collected in writing – the Scripture. The Apostles were the inspired interpreters of the faith, so we want to understand what they taught the first Christians.

The earliest sermons of the Apostles give us a quick insight into Apostolic teaching. (See Peter's sermons in Acts 2:14-36; Acts 3:12-26; Acts 4:8-12; Acts 5:29-32; and the sermon of Stephen in Acts 7:2-56.) In summary these sermons say:

1) The time of fulfillment has come
2) The Messiah has arrived in Jesus Christ
3) He was crucified for our sins, rose again and ascended to the Father
4) He will come again to judge the world
5) Repent, turn to Jesus in faith, and be baptized.

It is certainly possible that Jesus covered this basic framework of thought with Cleopas. If so, it would account for his burning heart.

Today we are called to proclaim and recite God's great saving deed in our public worship. The presence of God is communicated to us in this historical recitation. When we proclaim God's great saving deeds in history, a divine action occurs. "The word of God," says the author of Hebrews, "is living and active. Sharper than any double-edged sword, it penetrates even to dividing soul and spirit, joints and marrow; it judges the thoughts and attitudes of the heart" (Hebrews 4:12). This divine action, this *something from above*, occurs through historical recitation.

Let me illustrate this truth with a story:

> *Some time ago, William Allen Farmer, African-American songwriter/worship leader, came to Wheaton College to give some lectures on worship. His first lecture was titled "He is an Awesome God!" He asked the students, "How do you know that God is an awesome God?" He answered his own question this way: You know God is awesome when you recite God's great deeds in history. Then he said, "You'll*

53

*never go to one of our African-American churches without hearing the recitation of God's great deeds in history." He told the story then in a way I can't, but basically he said: "There were the people of Israel in bondage to Pharaoh, making bricks without straw, crying out to God to deliver them. And God sent Moses and with signs and wonders delivered them. And there are Shadrach, Meshach, and Abednego in the fiery furnace. God met them and delivered them. There's Daniel in the lion's den, and God met him and shut the mouths of the lions.*

*"You know what happens when you recite God's great deeds in history? You identify with the message. You listen and say, 'Yeah, that's me! I'm there with Daniel. And if God can do that in Biblical history, He can do that today.'"*

That's our experience. It's an experience of confidence in the God of Scripture. It's the "yes" to the presence of God, working in our lives right now. We certainly see this pattern in Cleopas. After Jesus explained the Scriptures, there was a burning response of "yes" in his heart.

Through this pattern we link the God who was active in Biblical times with the God who is active in our lives, active in our families, active in our churches, and active in our nation. When we have been able to identify our brokenness and our dislocations, and we let God speak to us through the recitation of His saving deeds in history, *we come out on the other side* – into our relocation in God. It is here that we experience the presence of the saving and healing God, and we respond with praise. God has acted. We have responded. That's public worship... the presence of God in the Word.

54

## A Biblical Example of the Presence of God in the Word

The most striking example of an encounter with God through the Word is found in Nehemiah chapter 8. Briefly, the setting is this: The Israelites were returning from their exile in Babylon. They set out to rebuild Jerusalem and in the process found the book of the law of Moses. Ezra called them all to assemble in Jerusalem to hear the word of God. The account is rather long, so I have selected excerpts to give us the sense of what happened:

> "...All the people assembled as one man in the square before the Water Gate. They told Ezra the scribe to bring out the Book of the Law of Moses, which the Lord had commanded for Israel... He read it aloud from daybreak till noon... and all the people listened attentively... [He] stood on a high wooden platform built for the occasion... Ezra opened the book. All the people could see him... as he opened it, the people stood up. Ezra praised the Lord, the great God; and all the people lifted their hands and responded, "Amen! Amen!" Then they bowed down and worshiped the Lord with their faces to the ground... They read from the Book of the Law of God, making it clear and giving the meaning so that the people could understand what was being read... Then all the people went away to eat and drink... because they now understood the words that had been made known to them" (Nehemiah 8:1-12).

There are several very striking features of this event. First, you'll notice in the unabridged passage that the word *assemble* or *assembly* is used several times in the text. Next comes the reading of the Word. Significant meaning is attached to the raising up of Scripture, to the attentiveness of the people, to standing in the presence of the Word, to the lifting of hands, to the bowing of the head, to the clarity of meaning, and to an understanding by the people. Then note, the people went away to eat and drink. In addition, I did not quote this part in the text, but we are told that they were to "proclaim this word and spread it throughout their towns and in Jerusalem" (8:15). Here is the fourfold pattern of worship:

- Assemble (Gather)
- Hear the word
- Celebrate with eating, praise, and thanksgiving
- Go forth to live the life and tell others.

What does all of this mean for us *today* in our journey into the presence of God at the Word?

## The Word of God Today

We have seen that divine action always comes first. And then our response, which is our experience, is second. The Scripture is read first, then we respond. We saw this pattern in Ezra, and we can see this pattern in the earliest noncanonical description of the service of the Word, written by Justin Martyr at 150 A.D.

> And on the day called Sunday, all who live in cities or in the country gather together to one place, and the memoirs of the Apostles or the writings of the prophets are read, as long as time permits; then when the reader has ceased, the president [minister] verbally instructs, and exhorts to the limitation of these good things. Then we all rise together and pray. (Justin Martyr, first apology, 67).[1]

---

[1]Taken from Cyril Richardson, *The Early Christian Fathers,* (Philadelphia: The Westminster Press, 1963), p.287.

Both the description of God's presence in the Word by Ezra and the description of early Christian worship by Justin say two very clear things to us: We need to improve our experience of *reading* the Word; we need to improve our experience of *hearing* the Word.

## Improve the Experience of Reading the Word

We need to approach the public sharing of the Word today against the background of the history of communication. In Biblical times people communicated in the form of stories that were told and retold and handed down intact. During the medieval period there was a shift into visual forms of communication; people were basically illiterate, and so in church buildings the Gospel was illustrated on the walls of the church. We still see examples of this visual form if we go into an Orthodox church or a Catholic church. The entire Gospel is presented in the icons, the frescoes, the stained glass windows, and the artwork.

The 15th century experienced a great communication revolution with the invention of the Gutenburg press. Since the invention of the press made print available, the Renaissance brought education back into being. With the Word now available in written form and with literacy on the rise, inspiration struck many reformers that the Bible should be translated into modern languages.

One such reformer was Huldrych Zwingli, the pastor of a church in Zurich. This church had been a Catholic church, but it became a Reformed church during the time of the Reformation. Zwingli ordered his people to whitewash the church, eliminating the visuals inherited from the Medieval period. His belief was that the church should be Word-driven, and gathering around the visuals was, therefore, a false doctrine.

To emphasize this point, he took a Bible, opened it, and placed it on the table in the midst of the congregation saying, "Here is what we gather around – the Bible."

The Reformation left us this legacy: for the next 400 years, Protestants became primarily Word-driven in worship. However, in the last half of the twentieth century, there has been an incredible communications revolution. People have been saying, "I want to *see* to understand also." Suddenly we're in an audiovisual revolution.

Those concerned with the form of the worship service and ministry are asking, "How do we make the Service of the Word more audiovisual in a society that demands a visual sense as well as verbal sense?"

We are all aware that communication of the Word of God is essential to worship. There is no such thing as full worship without the presence of God communicated to us in the reading and preaching of the Word. For this reason, there are several matters we must address in order to encounter the presence of God at the Word. What we learn from Ezra, Cleopas, and Justin Martyr is the need to have *more Scripture, not less*.

It concerns me that in many churches I have visited recently, there is no Bible reading at all. In fact, while I was traveling in Fargo, North Dakota, a young man came to me with a problem. He said, "Bob, I'm in big trouble in the church!"

I asked him, "How so?"

He responded, "The minister has told us we're going to go seeker-sensitive; no more Bible-reading, no more intercessory prayer, no more anything that might offend the seeker."

**58**

Obviously, this church took a ridiculous stand. Why else are seekers there? But I'd like to look at another aspect of this issue.

Part of the problem is that Scripture is often not presented well. We need to change that. From my experience in visiting many churches, I can see that a common element for improvement would be to ensure that we have *good* reading of the Word. Have you ever been in a worship community where the reading was done so well that you just sat up at attention and listened to it? Unfortunately, in most churches I have visited, the reading is more or less mumbled. My first suggestion for enhanced communication would be for each church to begin a *lay readers' group.* Every church has people within the community who are good communicators. Once those having this gift are identified, they could be brought together into a lay readers' group. This would also return reading to the people, where it belongs. It's not the pastor's job to read the Scripture. That's a clericalization of worship.

These lay readers would gather together during the week, read to each other, pray through the Scriptures, and seek to understand the Scripture. In that way, when they stand up and read the Scripture, the reading will be *clear* and *proclamatory.* The Word will be communicated well and the people will have opportunity to participate actively in the worship service. These same people would be responsible for drama and *storytelling*[2] of the Gospel, two forms of communication that are now being well received in worship.

## Improve the Experience of Hearing the Word

I am impressed by the response of the people in the Ezra account of reading and preaching God's Word. They listened

---

[2]Example: Remember my paraphrasing the story of Cleopas.

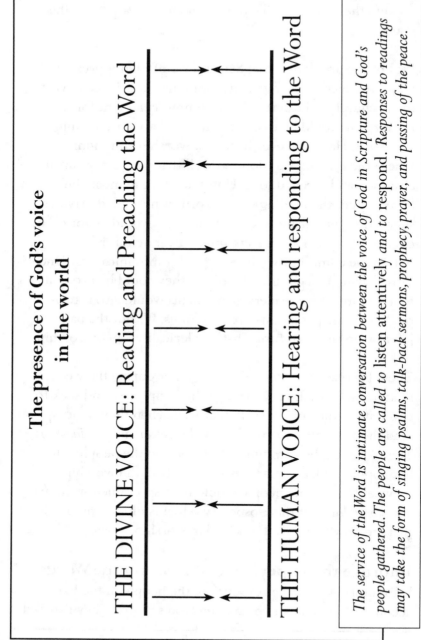

The presence of God's voice in the world

THE DIVINE VOICE: Reading and Preaching the Word

THE HUMAN VOICE: Hearing and responding to the Word

*The service of the Word is intimate conversation between the voice of God in Scripture and God's people gathered. The people are called to listen attentively and to respond. Responses to readings may take the form of singing psalms, talk-back sermons, prophecy, prayer, and passing of the peace.*

Figure 5

60

attentively, they stood, they said, "Amen", they raised their hands and bowed their heads.

I am also impressed by the insight we have on early Christian worship at the Word in Justin and other sources. They apparently sang psalms between readings, discussed the readings, and stood for the reading of the Gospel. They generally listened attentively and even responded out loud to the reading of Scripture and to preaching. Also, for them, the time of prayer was always in response to the Word.

What can we learn about our journey into the presence of God from these sources?

My suggestion is that we become more intentional in hearing the divine voice and in responding with the human voice to the presence of God experienced in the reading and preaching of the Word. (See Figure 5.)

First, I suggest a public and communal response to the reading and to the sermon. Let me give you several examples. I often attend traditional worship and love the response to the reading of Scripture. It goes like this:

> reader: *This is the Word of God*
> people: *Thanks be to God* (with enthusiasm)

Here is another example: I was in a church in Russia some years ago. At the end of a moving and heartfelt sermon, the people immediately and spontaneously cried "thank you" (in Russian, of course).

It doesn't matter what language you thank the Lord in so long as it is truly a heartfelt cry, as was the case with this Russian congregation. We can experience the presence of God through our *response* to Scripture reading and preaching.

Another way to increase attention to the Word is to sing after a reading. The choir could, for example, sing the verse of a song or psalm and then the congregation could sing the refrain; or the people could sing a contemporary psalm chorus or an *Alleluia!* song. All these forms of music increase our attention to the Word and allow us to interact with God's message to us.

I also advocate the return to the *talk-back sermon*. In early Protestant services of the 17th and 18th centuries, they spent a good thirty minutes discussing the Scripture reading and the message. A current adaptation of this practice would be for the pastor at the close of the sermon to invite the congregation, "Take two minutes to turn to one another and share what you heard, saw, felt, and experienced in the reading of the Word and the sermon."

An important benefit of this talk-back concept is that communication specialists tell us we take home more of what we *said* than what we *heard*. Therefore, in the context of a sermon, what we filter through our minds and speak about to other people is what we'll take home for reflection.

A further suggestion for increasing attentiveness and participation is to return prayer to the people. Interestingly enough, there was no such thing in the Early Church as a pastoral prayer. While we don't want to take that element away from the pastor who prays very well, the Early Church is replete with alternatives. One practice is called bidding prayers. For example, if the leader says: "I bid you to pray for the sick," the worshipers then pray the first name or names of those they know who are sick: "*Bill, Harry, June, Sally.*"

(We need to be sensitive to the fact that this is a time of prayer. I wouldn't pray, *"Oh, Lord, you know how Sally was*

people are going to know God is a welcoming God is if we're a welcoming people."

I loved that explanation! I love anything that makes an implication of *incarnational faith*. He was definitely incarnating God's welcome. He then said to the people, "Peace be with you."

They responded, "And also with you." Then they broke out and passed the peace to everybody.

That church today is well over a thousand strong, and they now call their passing-of-the-peace time *Holy Bedlam*. They don't identify it in their bulletin as Holy Bedlam time, you understand. They label it *Passing of the Peace*, but their nickname gives you some understanding of the enthusiasm with which they celebrate this portion of the service.

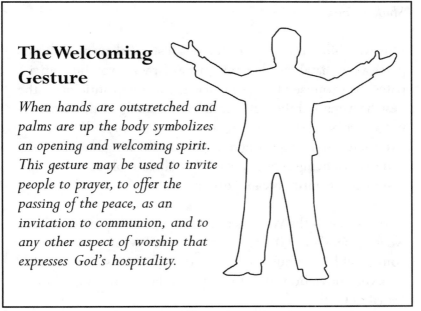

## The Welcoming Gesture

*When hands are outstretched and palms are up the body symbolizes an opening and welcoming spirit. This gesture may be used to invite people to prayer, to offer the passing of the peace, as an invitation to communion, and to any other aspect of worship that expresses God's hospitality.*

Figure 6

65

## Reconciliation

There's a second meaning to the passing of the peace. It has a kind of confessional nature to it. If you have something against your brother or sister, this provides you with the opportunity and the incentive to get it right before you come to the Table of the Lord.

## Christ's Peace

The last implication in the passing of the peace that I would like to bring to your attention is couched in highly theological terms: *it's a momentary experience of God's Shalom, the peace of God which will cover the whole earth.* An illustration may be the best way to develop this thought. For many years the Sherwin Williams company has used as part of their logo a picture of a large open paint can being tipped over a smaller scale planet earth. The paint is viewed as thickly covering most of the earth and dripping off, indicating a lavish and thorough supply. Every time I see or think of that, I say, "Aha! *Shalom* [peace] of God."

Our worship is not only rooted in a historical event, it anticipates an eschatalogical event: Just as Israel's worship anticipates the promised land, so Christian worship anticipates the new heavens and the new earth. The passing of the peace is not a secular, casual greeting. It's a true, deeply religious experience of being brought right into the kingdom of God and experiencing momentarily that Shalom of God that will rest over the entire created order.

The Service of the Word is not to be a passive portion of our worship services. We must move beyond what is familiar, comfortable, or undemanding in our traditions and actively seek the conviction, the stirring, and the challenging of the Word of God.

# Bringing Stage Two into Focus

Let's remember that our journey, whether personal or public, is directed toward a destination. In our journey we have come to a point where we need to stay awhile so that God can communicate to us and we to God.

The movement of our personal journey is therefore characterized by an inner dynamic of proclamation and response. This dynamic is also the public structure of the Word: God speaks — we respond.

This is certainly the case with Cleopas. He isn't a hesitant believer; our vision of him is that he readily hears the Word, receives it as truth, and resolves to live by it. This is the process of transformation, a process by which the presence of God in the Word takes up residence within us. You will know, better than anyone else, what word is knocking on the door of your heart saying, "Let me in." I can only encourage you, and myself as well, to be "obedient to that word" and so experience the direct and immediate presence of God in our lives.

In public worship, the presence of God in the Word comes to us through the reading of the Word and preaching. God makes Himself known to us as we recall His great saving actions in the past. These actions *continue in the present* in our own lives.

I think a lot of believers relegate God's active presence to the past. This probably comes from an unfortunate teaching that God ceased working in history after the coming of His Son. Nothing could be less true. The church is empowered by the Spirit to continually bring God's actions in our lives; the Spirit attends the reading of the Word and preaching; the

67

Spirit illumines us. Or, in more contemporary words, the Spirit is always giving us new insights, new *aha*'s!

Look for the presence of God in the Word. This presence will speak to the problems of your life; it will fill you with hope and give you meaning as you understand your place in life. It will also give you teaching in wisdom that will inform your behavior and empower your relationships.

The result of your participation in the Word will be this: Your response to God will be filled with greater intensity. Singing a psalm or singing an alleluia, responding to the sermon or passing the peace of Christ will be charged with emotion, expressed with sincerity. It will also confirm your belongingness to this local church community, to the Church around the world and throughout history, and to God who encounters you with His overwhelming presence.

It is equally important for us to recognize that God is forming a community of praise in the service of the Word. The Church is God's community in the world, a community that is called to be a sign of God's presence in the world. Consequently, it is God's intention that we should be shaped into Christ-likeness not only individually, but corporately.

We now turn to the most intense experience of the presence of God... the presence of Christ in our eating.

## How Far Have We Come?
- We must not only be open, but actually embrace the Word that God has for us
- We are supernaturally changed by the operation of the Word in us

- We become the temple of God as His Word dwells within us
- We are empowered by the recitation of God's mighty acts throughout history
- We need to read the Word more in our worship services – and read it well
- We assimilate more of what we actually speak as well
- We speak forth peace to others and find it a creative act

## Thinking It Over

1) Do you remember ever having a "burning heart" experience? Try to describe it.
2) Can you remember an experience of emotional or physical healing? Tell someone about it.
3) Give an example of one time when you "housed" the Word of God in your life.
4) Recall a time that you have intensely experienced the presence of God in reading and/or the preaching of the Word in worship.

# *tage Three of the Journey: The Lord Is Risen!*

*Their eyes were opened and they recognized him … when he broke the bread (Luke 24:31 and 35).*

It is really quite clear that the high point of the Cleopas story is the breaking of the bread. Until that moment Jesus remained hidden as the Christ, the son of the living God. However, we are justified in seeing an inner process of healing going on in the life of Cleopas. There are thresholds of insight as he travels on the road. He began in great despair; next the word of God touched him where he hurt and a transformation began; but it wasn't until Jesus lifted up the bread and broke it that Cleopas knew Jesus. The breaking of the bread was the most personal and intense encounter with the presence of God. It was the experience of coming into the holy of holies, the experience of entering into the very throne room of God – that place where God is present in all His overwhelming glory – and Cleopas was healed. He was a new man, born again. We want to explore this incredible mystery of how God becomes present at the table in our personal worship and in our corporate experience of worship.

## Our Personal Experience of the Presence of God in the Breaking of the Bread

The experience of breaking bread together in a special meal goes back to the Jewish *Shabbat,* the opening meal on the Friday night of the Sabbath. I want to explore what significance the breaking of the bread may have had for Cleopas, a Jew. A good illustration comes from a personal experience I had at a Shabbat meal in the home of an orthodox rabbi.

> *I was involved in a dialogue between a group of Protestant professors and a group of Jewish rabbis. We met together once a month for an exchange of ideas and for fellowship. In this context I became good friends with one of the rabbis: Rabbi Yechiel Eckstein. One day after our group dialogue, Rabbi Yechiel said to me, "Would you and your wife come to our house on Friday night for our Shabbat meal?" I'll tell you one thing, when an orthodox rabbi invites you to his home for a Shabbat meal, you don't hesitate. You quickly clear the calendar and answer, "Yes."*
>
> *Rabbi Yechiel then wrote directions to his home and handed them to me and to another of my colleagues whom he had invited. Then he said, "Don't lose these directions. After dusk on Friday night we don't answer the phone. As a matter of fact, we don't do any work for twenty-four hours." The thought quickly ran through my Protestant-work-ethic mind, "Oh, to be a Jew!"*
>
> *We arrived at his house at the appointed time, knocked on the door, and waited only a few seconds before his wife opened the door. With a burst of energy and with a warm welcoming smile she said, "Hi, I'm Bonnie. Welcome to our home. Please come in." As we entered the house, she pointed to eight burning candles. "You see those candles?" she asked. "Each candle represents one of the eight people here*

*tonight: four for our family, four for you." I felt very welcomed.*

*For the next thirty minutes or so, we engaged in small talk, getting acquainted with each other. We were given a quick tour of their home, stopping here and there to admire a picture or an antique.*

*Soon it was time for dinner. Yechiel announced, "The table is ready. Come, let's eat." We all gathered around the table and stood behind our assigned chairs. On the table in front of Yechiel was a bottle of wine and a freshly baked loaf of bread. Yechiel, pointing to the bread and the wine, said: "It is a Jewish tradition to give thanks for the produce of the earth and the fruit of the vine with the symbols of bread and wine." He then took the bread into his hands, lifted it for all to see, and prayed the ancient Jewish table prayer thanking God for the gifts of the earth. He broke the bread and passed it around for each of us to eat. Next he lifted the cup and prayed the ancient Jewish prayer thanking God for the fruit of the vine. Then he poured the wine into eight cups, passed them to us, and we all drank. Following that little ceremony, we sat down to eat.*

*I love to eat. I especially love to eat good food in the context of a lively and stimulating conversation. That is exactly what was happening during that meal. The food tasted delicious. The communication between us was full of life. Strong emotional connections were being established. After the meal was over, Rabbi Yechiel informed us that the Jewish Shabbat ended with a psalm which he and his wife would sing together in an antiphonal manner. They sang the song in the Hebrew language, and as it was being sung we were drawn into the spirit of its rejoicing. When the psalm was finished, Yechiel looked across the table and told his wife in no uncertain terms how fortunate he was to have her as his wife; how he thanked God for her; what a joy she was to his life; what a wonderful mother she was to her children; what an excellent cook and outstand-ing hostess she was. Then he invited his children to come and stand before him. Placing his right hand on the top of the head of the first, then the second child, he prayed a special prayer of blessing over each. They ran off to play, and shortly thereafter we got into our car for our return trip to Wheaton.*

*I was in the back seat. I don't think we had gone a few blocks before I said, "Whew! That was a great evening!" Of course everybody else agreed. We then began to explore what it was that made the evening so special. I recalled a comment Yechiel made to me that evening. "You know, Bob," said Yechiel, "we Jews just love the Sabbath. It's a time to put aside our work and concentrate on relationships — relation-ships with God, with our family, and with those whom we love." We began to explore this idea and came to the conclusion that our time together around the table was so significant because it was the context in which relationships were affirmed and developed.*

Now let's go back to the breaking of the bread in the Cleopas story. What happened when Jesus broke the bread? Immedi-ately in that moment the relationship was affirmed between

73

Cleopas and Jesus. Cleopas knew Jesus in the breaking of the bread.

The personal dimension of this experience runs down two roads. The first road takes us into all experiences of eating together. When we eat with family or friends or strangers, the dynamics of the meal include the personal relationship that is developing around food.

The fact that relationships are nourished and intensified through our eating together leads me to this observation: Christianity is, in some ways, a food-driven faith. (We lost the closeness of our relationship with God over food!) In Biblical history, food is always involved in the presence of God. He established feast days as commemorations of miraculous events in His dealings with the children of Israel. He came to us in Jesus Christ as the *Bread of Life.* In eating, both our common everyday eating and our special time of eating in public worship, we are drawn into the intensity of our relationship with the presence of God. Actually, God is present in all our eating and may be experienced in the relationships being nurtured through all our meals with those we love and with those whom we meet on occasion. Indeed, God was present in our eating at the home of Rabbi Yechiel. It was both a vertical and horizontal presence.

The second road is that special – very special – experience of eating at the table of the Lord in public worship. Let's turn to an examination of this experience.

## Our Corporate Experience of the Presence of God in Worship

Worship at the Table was normative in the Early Church. The worship of the early Christians drew from two sources: Their experience in synagogue worship, with its emphasis on reading and responding to the Word, influenced their gathering at the Word; the institution of the Lord's supper as well as the Friday night *Shabbat* (Sabbath) meal influenced their worship at the Table. (See Figure 7.)

## The Biblical Foundations

This pattern of worship first began as new Jewish Christians stayed in the synagogue but celebrated the breaking of the bread in the fellowship of a Christian home (Acts 2:42-47). Gradually, as Christianity spread, the new Christians left the synagogue and met in house church settings where they heard the Word and celebrated at the Table. In Justin Martyr's second century description of worship he informs us:

> [After scripture, sermon, prayer, and passing of the peace] bread and wine and water are brought, and the president [minister] in like manner offers prayers and thanksgiving, according to his ability, and the people assent saying Amen; and there is a distribution to each, and a participation of that over which thanks have been given, and to those who are absent a portion is sent by the deacons (First apology of Justin, 67).

From the time of Justin and the Early Church all the way into the Medieval Era, the Church celebrated both Word and Table every time it gathered together to worship. In the late medieval period, the Church fell away from the celebration of the Word and worshiped only with the Eucharistic mass. The Reformers of the Church, wanting to go back to the Biblical and Early Church tradition, declared: "We want to return to the balance of Word and Table." The writings of Luther, Calvin, Zwingli, and of Anabaptists share this common theme: They wanted to recover what was true in the Early Church. Today our calling is to return to the model of the

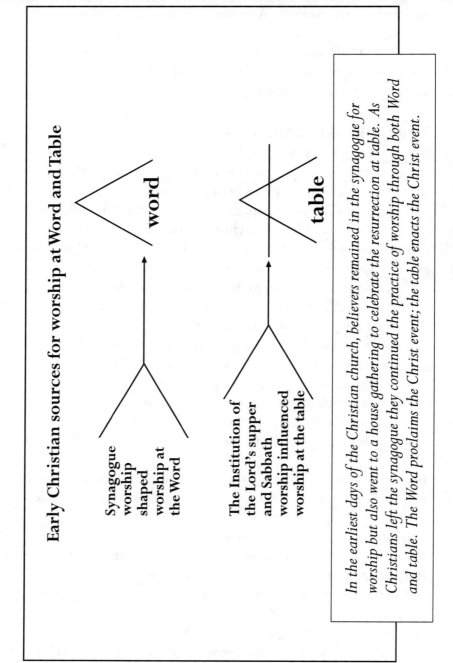

# Early Christian sources for worship at Word and Table

**word**

Synagogue
worship
shaped
worship at
the Word

**table**

The Institution of
the Lord's supper
and Sabbath
worship influenced
worship at the table

*In the earliest days of the Christian church, believers remained in the synagogue for worship but also went to a house gathering to celebrate the resurrection at table. As Christians left the synagogue they continued the practice of worship through both Word and table. The Word proclaims the Christ event; the table enacts the Christ event.*

*Figure 7*

Early Church: *proclaim* the Word through Scripture and *enact* the Word at the Table.

If the Reformers were right in calling for Word and Table, then we must ask why. Why should we celebrate the Table on a regular, perhaps even weekly basis?

An answer to this question arises out of our understanding of the four terms used in Scripture to describe Table worship. It is the *Lord's Supper* (I Corinthians 11:20), the *Breaking of Bread* (Acts 2:42), *Communion* (I Corinthians 10:16), and *Eucharist* (I Corinthians 14:16). A brief examination of each of these terms will help us grasp what lies at the heart of God's intense presence at the Table.

The oldest of these terms is the *Breaking of the Bread*. To understand the experience of the early Christians, we go back to the Friday night *Shabbat* (Sabbath) meal and to its twenty-four hour period of rest. What Jews love about the Sabbath is that it is a day to set aside all work and enjoy their relationship with God and each other. Consequently, *when the early Christians came to Table worship, they came expecting a relationship with the resurrected Christ.* As Christ became present in the breaking of the bread on the Emmaus road (Luke 24), so they anticipated *the real presence* of Jesus in their midst, communicated through bread and wine. This was a great experience of joy, an experience that is still available today!

In 57 A.D. Paul wrote to the troubled church of Corinth and used a second image, the *Lord's Supper*. He was addressing some very real problems as to how they were handling the celebration of the Table of the Lord. He told them to stop getting drunk and to remember the needs of the poor. It seems clear that Paul was stern because they were turning

77

celebration of the Table of the Lord into a gluttonous orgy. We know that the earliest purpose of Table worship was to celebrate the resurrection of Christ. But now Paul shifted the emphasis to the death – a sobering thought which we Western Christians have universalized. In many of our churches we only remember the death and fail to celebrate the resurrection!

The third image of Table worship is the term *Communion*. Scholars generally agree that this is a reference to what is called a *covenant meal*. Looking through the Bible, all of the covenants – the agreements between God and God's people – are characterized by meals. Why? A meal is the sign of relationship. During meals relationships are established, strengthened, maintained, repaired, and transformed. What happens, therefore, at the Communion Table is the intensification of relationship with Jesus at bread and wine.

For example, remember how you felt when beginning a new relationship, perhaps when you were in college? You were walking across the campus one day and saw a very attractive member of the opposite sex? You said to yourself, "Oooooooh! La, la!" You managed to meet this person and offered to carry her books to class – or if you're a female, you suggested studying together. The relationship stayed at this level for some time until finally you decided to "make your move."

You asked, "Could we have dinner together?"

We all know that eating together puts a relationship into a different setting. If you want to get to know someone, you want to eat with them. Eating is the context for developing relationships, and that's exactly what happens in the Communion.

78

A fourth insight into Table worship is revealed through the word *Eucharist* — a Greek word meaning *to give thanks*. Through our celebration we offer our thanks to God for His work of salvation within history. This element of thanks is our response. It is the experience of gratitude and joy. For this reason, the prayer said over the bread and wine is called *thanksgiving*. More about that later.

There is no other experience in worship that can equal the intensity of Table worship. We literally enter into the unrepeatable historic event of the death and resurrection of Jesus, and our life in faith is empowered by the pattern of death and resurrection. We intentionally unite with Jesus when we ingest the bread and wine which are the very symbols of His life-giving power. All our deaths, our distractions, our frustrations, our brokenness, our pain, our sins are mystically united with the death of all deaths. We are raised in newness of life through the resurrection of Jesus with whom we are joined. Having communed with Him, we go forth with an eternal "Thank You" on our lips. This was the experience of Cleopas and the experience of millions who have known Jesus in the breaking of the bread.

Here, without question, is the climactic point of our worship. Talk about presence! This is not only presence, but a joining with presence, an experience of the Holy Other who became one of us to deliver us from all that is sin and death in this world.

## How Is This Experience Ordered for Us?

The order of the experience is very simple. We follow the pattern of Jesus in the home of Cleopas. "When He was at the Table with them, He took bread, gave thanks, broke it and began to give it to them" (Luke 24:30).

79

Let's explore this fourfold structure for its content, for what it says to us about our worship, and how it shapes our experience. (See Figure 8.)

---

• Begin with a song inviting people to come to Communion.
  During the singing have the bread and wine brought to the table by a family.

• Pray a prayer of thanksgiving that
  praises the Father
  thanks the Son
  invokes the Holy Spirit.
  (This prayer may be sung using contemporary songs, or insert a song after each of the three parts of prayer.)
  End with the words of Institution (on the night, etc... )

• Invite the people to walk forward to receive the bread and wine.

As people come to receive, sing praise and thanksgiving songs that carry the people through the
  Death
  Resurrection
  Intimacy
  Thanksgiving.

At the same time offer prayers with the anointing of oil and the laying on of hands.

• Linger in the presence. Then close with a song or prayer.

---

*Figure 8*

# The Taking

The *taking* refers to the setting of the Table. In most Protestant churches, the Table is set before worship begins; however, many renewing churches are no longer preparing the bread and the wine before worship begins. The reason is that preparation prior to worship constitutes a mixture of symbols. The dominant symbol for the Word is the Bible; the dominant symbol for Communion is the bread and wine.

Here's the problem: If you put the bread and wine on the Communion Table, even if it's covered, the moment a worshiper walks into the church he begins to focus on Communion. Even the pastor will think, "I've got to preach something about Communion... I need to preach a meditation on the death."

Consequently the Communion theme is pushed into the service of the Word and, in some cases, even into the Gathering. When this happens the integrity of the Gathering — *which is to assemble* — and the integrity of the Word — *which is to communicate God's truth for our lives* — is violated. Each part of worship needs to stand on its own, interlocked with the other stages of the journey, but not intermeshed with or eclipsed by other stages.

Here is one way to solve the problem: During the service of the Word, have an open Bible on the Table. After the service of the Word, remove the Bible and have a family bring the bread and wine. In this way the *taking* occurs at the appropriate time. The symbolism of setting the Table as a response to the Word will also communicate the shift from hearing God's Word to responding with praise and thanksgiving at the Table.

81

In many churches, a song about coming to Communion is sung as the taking or bringing of the bread and wine to the table occurs.

## The Blessing

Almost every church has a blessing of some sort for this time of Holy Communion. To provide you with an example, let me take you down to the Ozarks to a little clapboard church with 12 people in it:

> The pastor's going to say, "Brother Brown, would you lead us in a prayer thanking God for the Bread?"
>
> Brother Brown will say, "Lord, we give You thanks for Your death and resurrection, Your broken body for us."
>
> This is a progressive church, so he says, "And Sister Smith, would you please give us a prayer over the wine?" And Sister Smith will pray something very similar, emphasizing the shed blood.

## The Threefold Thank-You Prayer

Most churches have a thank-you prayer. Let's take a little time to understand its origin and its meaning.

The origin of the *thank-you prayer* goes back to the Hebrew *berakah* prayers. *Berakah* prayers were blessing prayers, which is what the word means. And all *berakah* prayers are ordered around **praise, commemoration,** and **petition.**

Here's an example:

> Blessed be God [praise] who brought us out of Egypt [commemoration], bringing us to the promised land [petition].

82

This is a *berakah* prayer, a blessing. What is important for us to notice is that it was the *berakah* prayer that influenced the shape of the thank-you prayer in the Early Church. In the historic prayer of thanksgiving, we *praise the Father, thank the Son, and invoke the presence of the Holy Spirit.* Let's examine each of these aspects of prayer.

## Praise to the Father

First, praise to the Father. Historic worship begins:

> *Leader: Lift up your hearts!*
> *People: We lift them to the Lord.*
> *Leader: Let us give thanks to the Lord, our God.*
> *People: It is right to give Him thanks and praise.*

You know what this prayer and response is saying? It's saying, "Go! Get you up into the Heavens!" It's another ascent! The journey of worship now continues up into the heavenlies and before the very throne of God.

Now the minister will pray a short prayer ending with these words:

> *Therefore, joining with angels and archangels,*
> *cherubim and seraphim, and the whole company of*
> *saints, we forever sing:*

Then the congregation joins the heavenly throng and sings the Sanctus — "Holy, Holy, Holy" — the eternal and never-ending song (Revelation 4:8). Keep in mind that God loves to be worshiped. This is a foreign idea to us because of our natures. But here is a graphic illustration to help us understand what it means for God to love to be worshiped:

Let's say that somebody comes to you in the near future and says, "You know, I want to share something with you."

83

"Go ahead," you respond.

"I just want you to know that you're the most perfect person I've ever met in my life. I worship you, I adore you, I hymn you, I bless you, I fall before you."

Now, what are you going to say? I brought up this example in one of my classes a few years ago, and a woman in the back row hollered, "I'd marry him!"

Actually, most of us tend to recoil at that fervent kind of language. We'd say, "No, no, no, no, no...uh, uh, uh, uh, uh, uh...no, I'm just a creature like everybody else!" And that would be the appropriate response for us.

Now, let's go before the face of God. We ascend up into the Heavens around the throne of God with the angels and the archangels, and we cry, "Holy, holy, holy! Lord God of Sabaoth, the whole earth is full of Your Glory! I worship You, I adore You, I hymn You, I bless You, I fall before You!"

What do you think God's going to do? Do you think God is going to hang His head, shuffle His feet in celestial dust, and say, "Aw, shucks, don't do that!" Of course not because it's true! God loves to be worshiped in spirit and in truth.

When we worship God in truth, we put the world in order. We put God in God's place, and we see ourselves in our place. Through praise, we really *experience* the transcendence and the otherness of God.

## Thank You to the Son

Following the praise, in our threefold pattern of prayer, the second portion — *commemoration* — is primarily a historical recitation but with symbolic enactment. We thank the Son in words and with the drama of enactment that takes place in the "thank-you" prayer.

For example, here is a portion of the prayer that expresses that sense of thanksgiving for the saving work in history: It is the earliest known "thank-you" prayer. It was written down in about 215 A.D., but it is traceable to the *Berakah* prayers of the earlier Jewish tradition:

> *We render thanks (Eucharist) unto You, O God*
> *through Your beloved child Jesus Christ...You sent*
> *Him from heaven into the virgin womb, He was*
> *conceived in her womb and made flesh and was*
> *demonstrated to be Your Son being born of the Holy*
> *Spirit and a virgin. Who fulfilling Your will and*
> *preparing for You a Holy people, stretched forth His*
> *hands to voluntary suffering that He might release*
> *from suffering those who have believed in You. And*
> *when He was betrayed to voluntary suffering that*
> *He might destroy death and break the bonds of the*
> *devil and tread down hell, enlighten the righteous,*
> *fix the limit [of evil] and shine upon the*
> *righteous...He took bread and made Eucharist*
> *(adapted from Hippolytus, The Apostolic Tradition*
> *circa 215 A.D.).*[1]

Go back over the prayer and think through what it says. It is the chief act of praise and thanksgiving. It recites salvation history and cries thank you, thank you, thank you!

## O Holy Spirit, Come

The third part of the prayer said over bread and wine is the element of *petition*. This part of the prayer is directed toward

---

[1] R.C.D. Jasper and G.J. Cumings, *Prayers of the Eucharist: Early and Reformed,* (New York, Oxford University Press, 1980), p. 22.

the Holy Spirit. Again, let me quote from our third century manuscript, *The Apostolic Tradition.*

> *And we pray You to send Your Holy Spirit upon*
> *Your Holy Church. Grant to all who partake to*
> *be united to you so that they may be filled with*
> *the Holy Spirit for the confirmation of their faith*
> *in truth (Ibid).*

This part of the prayer is saying, *"O Holy Spirit, fall upon us, gather us into the unity of the Church, and confirm our faith by Your presence."*

## Relationship with the Triune God

Go back and reflect on this prayer and it will be obvious that it is a prayer which expresses relationship.

We enter into a relationship with the Father through praise: by speaking to God of God's worth. We enter into relationship with the Son by remembering the work of the Son with our thank you. We enter into relationship with the Holy Spirit through our prayers of petition, calling upon the Holy Spirit to become present.

Look at what's happening in the Eucharistic prayer. It's the most intense time of relationship. It's the Holy of Holies. It's entering into that point of time when the presence of Christ among us is heavy.

To further fasten in your mind the concept of praise, commemoration, and petition, I'd like to give you an assignment. Think right now about a person you really care about. This person could be a spouse, a child, a parent, or a good friend. Call or see this person and tell them *all the things you really like about them.*

Here's an example:

> "These are all of the things that I really like about you. You're honest, you're caring, you're considerate."

Then *thank the person* for all the things he or she does for you:

> "Once again, I just want to thank you for all the things you've done for me. You always remember me, you buy little gifts for me, and you do things for me when I am in need."

Follow this by saying, "Let's get together because *I would just like to be with you.*"

You can see the Trinitarian structure of worship developed through this exercise. We praise the Father, we thank the Son, and we call upon the presence of the Holy Spirit. There's an analogy between our human relationships and our relationship with God which is too often disregarded. Sometimes we make our relationship with God too abstract, pious, and therefore unreal. Just as we relate to another person on the basis of praise, thanks, and presence, so we relate to God in the same way. At the Table we enter into the most intimate relationship with God. Here is intensity. Here is overwhelming presence. Here the great mystery of our relationship to God is taking form.

I suggest that every church restore the Prayer of Thanksgiving. Let me give you an example.

> *Not long ago, I was giving some lectures to the Southern Baptists at a convention in South Carolina. We ended the lectures with a fourfold pattern of worship. I was assisted by a pastor I hadn't met before, who was to celebrate the Table of the Lord. In preparation, I asked him whether he wanted me to*

*give him any more information than what he had heard in my lecture about the praise, commemoration, and petition-for-presence prayer.*

*"Nah," he said, "I've got it!" I have to tell you that within myself I just thought, "Yeah...we'll see!" I was very skeptical.*

*As it turned out, I shouldn't have been. In fact, I should have a recording of his prayer. Here's a man who, without any written preparation or written prayers, prayed a very powerful prayer boasting in the worth of God. He continued with a very deeply moving thank-you prayer for the work of Christ, and closed with a passionate petition for the Holy Spirit to fall upon us, making us one and confirming within us our faith in Jesus.*

*Many Southern Baptists came up to me afterwards and said that was the "most significant Lord's Supper" that they had ever celebrated. They were moved to tears of joy. They had experienced a relationship with the living and life-giving triune God.*

## Breaking

After you've *Taken* and *Blessed*, you *Break*. I advocate that, when the breaking occurs, the bread be lifted high so that everybody can see it. It's very important to visualize the symbolic breaking of the bread. Let it be broken in a dramatic way. Sometimes we fear drama because we associate it with insincerity. That does not have to be the case. Everything in worship is essentially a form of drama, and we need to express it in that way. Take the bread and lift it high above your head so that everybody can *see* it, and if possible, even *hear* it as you break it. Attend the breaking with the words, "This is my body broken for you." Don't mutter these words; use your diaphragm and shout the words triumphantly.

Then there is the matter of wine. Here is another great and powerful symbol of the self-offering of Jesus on our behalf. Use a chalice, even if people are served with the little cups. Have the chalice positioned near the bread and have a silver pitcher full of wine or juice. Lift the pitcher high enough so that all may see it. Pour it into the chalice – not a trickle, but a *pour*. Make it dramatic and shout, "The blood of Christ shed for you." Then let the congregation burst out in song with a chorus like "Alleluia" by Jerry Sinclair or with "O the Blood of Jesus" (composer unknown). This is a moment of great drama, a moment that announces and demonstrates what is absolutely central to the Christian faith – a moment laden with emotional content. There is no missing of the moment when it is treated with the respect of high drama.

## Giving

After the breaking of the bread, the people *receive* the bread and wine. This is the act of *giving*.

We need to think about the giving/taking in terms of an axiom: *External action orders and organizes internal response.* For this reason, *it is important for us to come forward to receive.* I want you to know exactly what I'm challenging with this statement. I'm challenging the Protestant notion that comes out of the Puritan fathers and mothers that the bread and wine should be delivered to people in the pew. This is just too passive a method for a time when the congregation should be the most intimately and actively involved. The way for people to be involved is to have them stand up, walk to the front, receive the bread and the wine, and then go back to their pew. All of that activity is symbolic of positive commitment.

The walking to the front to receive says, "Yes!" Luther said that the promise is right there in bread and wine.[1] We walk forward to receive that promise in the same way we act to receive salvation. We internalize — we ingest it, and Christ is then within us. John Wesley spoke about the Table of the Lord as being an *ordinance of conversion*. While there are some people who may disagree with that statement, I think he makes a powerful point.

Suppose, for example, that you have seekers in your worship. (In all of our worship times we should have seekers.) An invitation can be given to the seekers on this order: "If you have been considering the Christian faith and your relationship to it, and today would publicly like to claim that you are embracing the Christian faith, then I invite you to come and receive, making the first act of your public proclamation the reception of Bread and Wine." This is what Wesley called the *converting ordinance*.[2]

The physical setting must be designed for the intentional and active movement that denotes reception. The bread may be served by a person located in the middle of the front of the church. Persons who are serving the wine may hold the chalices or smaller cups on either side. The community then walks forward, row by row, making two lines, all receiving the bread from the same person, the drink from one of the other persons, and then walking back to the pews. It is a

---

[1] For a general presentation of this principle, see *Lutherworks.* vol. 37 and *Word and Sacrament III,* (Philadelphia: Mohlenberg Press, 1961).
[2] For a discussion of this idea, see Ole E. Borgen, *John Wesley on the Sacraments* (Nashville: Abington Press, 1972) especially chapter 5.

living illustration of the words of a traditional hymn: "Just as I am without one plea, but that thy blood was shed for me." (Written by Charlotte Elliott in 1834.) (See Figure 9.)

While people are walking forward to receive, Communion songs are in order. Looking at the fourfold pattern, the music of the Gathering has been joyful, bringing us into close relationship with God. The music of the Service of the Word has been more meditative because that's a time of instruction and thinking; and that's why psalms are so appropriate at that

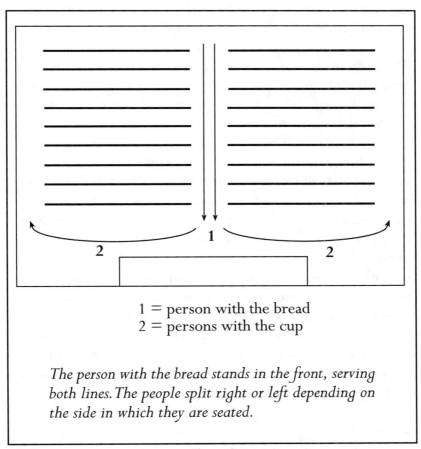

1 = person with the bread
2 = persons with the cup

*The person with the bread stands in the front, serving both lines. The people split right or left depending on the side in which they are seated.*

Figure 9

91

particular time. The music of the Table of the Lord is really quite unique because it carries us into the death, the resurrection, intimate relationship, and praise and thanksgiving. The singing of Communion songs challenges the funeral music used by so many of our churches. Too often we just play organ music or piano music, or some kind of instrumental music that's usually really quiet and meditative. We need to change that practice. Communion songs are the means by which we encounter mystery. Songs are, in a sense, the wheels upon which the rehearsal of our relationship with God occurs. Therefore, the songs at Communion need to fit the content of Communion. What is the content of Communion, and how can that be delivered through song?

The content of Communion is the Death, the Resurrection, Intimate Relationship, and Thank You. Our song time needs to lead us through this pattern of experience, for it is the shape of our relationship to God. For example, this is where choruses fit very well. Choose choruses that follow the path of remembrance of the death, celebration of the resurrection, entrance into intimate relationship, and a burst of thank-you praise. Be sure the words and sound fit together. If you have the right words but the wrong sound, the sound will always take away from the words, because sound is usually more powerful. For this reason, have a choir or worship leaders behind microphones to provide leadership for the congregation. Then tarry with these great songs. We don't want to rush through the Table of the Lord because this is where God is ministering to us. Lingering around the Communion Table and singing songs that rehearse the Christ event constitute the chief time of praise and thanksgiving in the entire time of worship.

Begin with a song that remembers the death. Hymns like George Bonnard's "The Old Rugged Cross" or a song from the Taizé community like "Jesus Remember Me" enter the death in both word and song. Then we shift into the resurrection. This shift is accomplished by a musical transition or by taking a few moments of silence to pause, change the mood, and then move into a resurrection song. The resurrection songs can be glorious musical expressions that gradually shift the focus more and more on the intimacy of relationship with God. These songs of intimacy will be quiet and meditative, giving the worshiper time to examine his or her relational needs with God.

Finally, close out the song time with a song of thanksgiving. As we joyfully embrace God's glorious gift of salvation, the music needs to be an explosive response of praise. Songs such as Graham Kendrick's "Shine, Jesus Shine" or Twila Paris' "He is Exalted" are two good examples of bursts of praise.[3]

## The Prayer for Healing

There's one more thing that is most appropriate to do at the time of the Eucharist: *prayers for healing.* Most renewal churches I have visited do this. The theological argument is that God does for us in worship what God did for us historically in Jesus Christ. Much of Jesus' ministry was devoted to healing: healing physical bodies, emotions, minds, and spirits.

One method of handling this healing time is to make an announcement to the people, via microphone or printed in the bulletin:

> *Are you struggling with anything in your life?*
> *Regardless of whether it involves a relationship*

---

[3]Note: I recommend *Renew! Songs and Hymns For Blended Worship* (Carol Stream, IL; Hope Publishing Co., 1995. This song book is organized around the fourfold pattern with extensive instructional notes and contains both old hymns and new choruses. Available through the Institute For Worship Studies.

*problem, finances, or emotional distress, we invite
you to come forward to receive the Eucharist and
God's healing. We also will anoint you with oil and
will pray for healing in your life.*

The congregation walks forward to receive the bread and the
wine, and those who desire prayer for healing will go to an
appointed place in the church (such as designated corners) to
receive prayer from those who minister the prayer for healing. The pray-er may take oil, and dip his/her thumb into it
and then splash it on the forehead of each person requesting
prayer.

I use the word *splash* because one of the things that's really
important, and will be increasingly important in the future, is
the more lavish nature of our symbols. We associate lavish
symbols with a lavish God. If we are stingy with our symbols,
people get a concept of a stingy God. Because of this associa-
tion, churches must also supply lots of bread, lots of wine,
and lots of oil. During the prayer for healing, oil is put on the
forehead in the name of the Father, Son, and Holy Spirit,
using the sign of the cross. Next the pray-er may put his or
her hands around each person's ears and just simply pray an
appropriate prayer, such as the following:

*May the Holy Spirit bring healing into your life —
mind, body, and soul. And may you be filled with
the presence of God.*

Once the prayer for healing is completed, the pray-er blesses
each departing person, sharing a passing of the peace.

I find that when I hold a workshop followed by a worship
service that incorporates a time of prayer for healing, about
80% of the people in attendance come forward to receive the
healing via laying on of hands. I've received many letters

following these workshops, particularly from ministers, which report the same basic response: "You know, nobody ever ministers to me, and I really *needed* that prayer of healing. It really ministered to me."

Notice the term: *ministry*. In worship, God ministers to us; and we respond with praise and thanksgiving, in essence, ministering to God in return.

## Bringing Stage Three into Focus

We have been on a journey into the presence of God. It is God who has called us to worship and assemble in His presence; it is God who has become present to us in the Word to instruct us concerning His saving ways in the world. And now, at the Table of the Lord, God calls us to respond. Of course, we have been responding throughout our journey, but here the journey has brought us into the throne room of God, the place of eternal worship with the angels, the archangels, the cherubim and seraphim, and with the whole company of saints, with whom we praise God, thank the Son and invoke the presence of the Holy Spirit. But alas! Communion is often missing in many of our Protestant churches. In some churches it is tacked on at the end of the service; in other churches its significance is not revered; and in many of our congregations, we simply don't understand it.

Let me tell you a story that will express my concern about the misunderstanding of Table worship. It's not my story, but it comes from a good friend of mine.

> *This friend, a bit of a mystic, started to have dreams of visuals and symbols that seemed to suggest he should find a new place of worship. After a time he became convinced that God was calling him to*

95

*become a member of a particular church in town. So he shared this information with his friends and they gave him a royal send-off to his new place of worship.*

*He loved this new church, the ardent singing, the good sermons, and the fellowship of the people. But he was curious about one thing: Why didn't they celebrate the Table of the Lord? After all, he had come from a church which celebrated the Table of the Lord regularly, and wasn't that a norm in worship?*

*Then, one Sunday after he and his family had been there for months, during the singing the worship leader said, "Oh, by the way, notice the table over there against the wall. It has some bread and juice on it. Go over there and help yourself and remember Jesus while we sing."*

*My friend was flabbergasted and promptly returned to his old church where Table worship was not a casual afterthought, but a vital part of weekly worship.*

From the perspective of Scripture and the Early Church, Table worship is an *essential* and not an incidental part of the journey into the presence of God. It brings public worship to its fulfillment and completion. It is the most intense experience of God's presence. It is the Holy of Holies of Christian worship.

Let's go back again to our story of Cleopas. It was at the Table, at the breaking of the bread, that Cleopas experienced the most intense relationship with God's presence. I think I know why we don't have this experience.

96

The major reason why we Protestants have ignored the presence of God at the Table is we really don't believe in an encounter with supernatural presence in the elements of bread and wine. We have dismissed this experience of worship as a mere memorial to be observed on occasion.

Of course, Jesus said, "Do this in remembrance of me" (I Corinthians 11:24). Our failure to interpret the word *remembrance* according to its original meaning is the culprit. We want to interpret the word to mean, "It's something I have to do. I have to exercise my mind and remember." I recall as a child when the words of communion were said: "This do in remembrance of me." I would close my eyes, squint into the darkness, and imagine Jesus on the cross between the two thieves. It was a thought process, a detached intellectual exercise. But that isn't what we are asked to do. We are asked to *re-member*. The original word has the force of action, not mere thought. The idea is "Go, get you to the assembly of Christians where you are membered together in the presence of Christ." Remembrance is a divine, spiritual, and mystical union with Christ, who is the head of the church, His body. In this act of gathering at the Table, the congregation is united as one in the body of Christ under the headship of Jesus Christ.

We have also, as Protestants, been inattentive to the presence of Christ by the power of the Holy Spirit in the elements themselves. I understand our rejection of the view that if we bite the bread, we have bitten the body. But we have pushed the symbol all the way over to the other end of the spectrum. We act as though the signs of bread and wine are empty symbols having no life-giving power. Follow this illustration that I often use with my students:

> I announce in class, "I've arranged for all of us to
> take a field trip to a satanic worship service. In this

97

*service they will slaughter a chicken, drain its blood into a cup, then cut the meat up in little pieces. The satanic minister will then hold his hands over the blood and chicken and consecrate these elements to Satan in prayer. And then he will invite us to drink the blood and eat the meat.*

*"Now," I say, "how many of you will go with me? Raise your hands."*

*There's never a one.*

*Then I say, "Good, I'm not going to go either. I certainly don't want to ingest evil into my life. I believe the prayer of consecration said by the satanic priest works in such a way that if I were to eat that meat consecrated in the name of Satan, I would really ingest the powers of evil. I don't want to eat and drink to the powers of evil. I don't want to ingest Satan into my life."*

*Then I say to students, "Look at the other side of the coin. We go to a Christian table service and the minister breaks the bread and raises the cup and prays a prayer of consecration, asking God to come upon this bread and wine and make it to be for us the body and blood of Jesus Christ our Savior. What's happening? Suppose the minister says, 'Now folks we don't believe in any kind of supernatural presence here, we're just remembering something from the past that really doesn't have any bearing on the present.' This would be an absolutely false statement."*

As in the story of Cleopas, there is a direct and meaningful encounter at bread and wine – the risen Christ meets us in all His glory and gives us a glimpse of what's to come.

If we fear the food consecrated in name of Satan, how much more should we embrace the food consecrated in the name of Jesus! There is no place in worship that is more intense, more filled with emotional content, more satisfying to the soul, than this union with the divine presence that meets us at bread and wine.

This is the missing jewel in many, many churches, but once we discover the power of worship at the Table, the jewel will be put back in its place of honor. God will be pleased, and the people will be filled with joy and great gladness of heart.

## How Far Have We Come?

- We have a personal and intense encounter with Christ in the Breaking of the Bread
- We find our relationship to Him nourished through this special meal
- We give thanks to God through this celebration of His provision for our salvation
- We find resurrection life in Communion
- We need to praise the Father, thank the Son, and petition the Holy Spirit to be present
- We must actively receive what He has provided
- We find healing on all levels during this stage of the journey

## Thinking It Over

1) Describe an enjoyable time you had recently sharing a meal with someone who is special to you.
2) How was your relationship in this setting either established, maintained, repaired, or transformed?

3) Describe the most powerful *Communion* experience in your memory.

4) How was Christ present to you in that communion?

# tage Four of the Journey: Go Forth!

*"They got up and returned at once to Jerusalem"*
*(Luke 24:33).*

There is an interesting and powerful inner development in the story of Cleopas. It moves from despair to a heart that is stirred into hope, and to an incredible climax of joyous transformation in the breaking of the bread. But the story, like worship, which rehearses God's work in history, doesn't stop there. It ends in action. We see two transformed lives, filled with the desire to go tell others.

I love the image of the text. What happened to Cleopas and his wife?

> Their eyes were opened
> They recognized Him
> They asked each other...
> They got up and returned at once to Jerusalem
> They found the eleven
> They said "It is true"
> They told others what had happened on the way

In terms of presence, how are we to understand the drive to go forth to tell others and how are we to live the life? The answer is found in the benediction. After Jesus ate with His disciples and instructed them, the text tells us that "He lifted up his hands and blessed them" (Luke 24:50).

101

## The Biblical Foundation

I have been surprised and somewhat dismayed to see that many churches no longer use the benediction. Worship is often closed with a prayer or a song. In these cases the people are missing the blessing God imprints on their lives as they go forth into the world of family living, leisure, work, and relationship with their neighbors.

The blessing or benediction originated in the Old Testament. It is an act of God that confers God's presence. It puts us under the blessing of God. Perhaps the most famous blessing is the Aaronic one:

> *The Lord bless you and keep you;*
> *the Lord make his face shine upon you*
> *and be gracious to you;*
> *the Lord turn his face toward you*
> *and give you peace (Numbers 6:24-26)*

It's hard for me to think that anyone would not *want* such a blessing. I want God to bless me in my family, in my relationships, in my work. I want God to keep me in the palm of His hand. I want God's face to shine upon me so that I may shine forth the love of God. I want God to be gracious to me, a sinner. I want God to turn His face toward me and assist me in doing what is right. I want God to fill my life with peace even in the midst of distractions, failures, and turbulence.

This blessing is one of presence. God's presence is within us and goes before us. It is the blessing that Joshua received before he led Israel into the promised land. God said to him, "As I was with Moses, so I will be with you; I will never leave you nor forsake you" (Joshua 1:5b). God's presence within us and upon us is not an occasional matter. It is a year-by-year, month-by-month, day-by-day, moment-by-moment experience. For us to know this and to live this way is revolutionary.

Here are the blessings found in the New Testament. Pray each one of them thoughtfully and meditate on the way in which each benediction invokes the presence of God upon you to go before you and lead you into the paths of righteousness.

Consider Philippians 4:7—

> *And the peace of God, which transcends all under-standing, will guard your hearts and your minds in Christ Jesus.*

Take time to pray Romans 15:13—

> *May the God of hope fill you with all joy and peace as you trust in him, so that you may overflow with hope by the power of the Holy Spirit.*

Reflect on the significance of I Thessalonians 5:23 (TEV)—

> *May the God of peace make you holy in every way and keep your whole being — spirit, soul, and body free from every fault at the coming of our Lord Jesus Christ.*

Meditate on Hebrews 13:20-21—

> *May the God of peace, who through the blood of the eternal covenant brought back from the dead our Lord Jesus, that great Shepherd of the sheep, equip you with everything good for doing his will, and may he work in us what is pleasing to him, through Jesus Christ, to whom be glory for ever and ever. Amen.*

If you go back over all these blessings, you will see that they confer on the recipient the presence of God in daily life; and what these blessings invoke upon us, we should *want:*

- the peace of God
- the knowledge of God
- the love of God
- the power of the Holy Spirit
- the blessing of God Almighty

Now go back and look at all the results that God will bring into your life because you have been blessed:

- make you holy in every way
- keep your whole being - spirit, soul, and body - free from every fault
- fill you with all joy and peace
- [make you] abound in hope
- make you complete in everything good
- enable you to do God's will
- [enable you to do] that which is pleasing in God's sight

## Our Personal Experience of the Presence of God in the Benediction

It is very clear from our brief inquiry into the benediction blessings that the presence of God is not only in public worship, but is supernaturally conferred on our lives as we go forth into the world to live out our worship.

Paul reminds us that all of life is worship. "Therefore, I urge you, brothers, in view of God's mercy, to offer your bodies as living sacrifices, holy and pleasing to God – which is your spiritual worship" (Romans 12:1).

This statement by Paul tells us *what* we are to do: We are to be motivated by the presence of God in our lives. Nevertheless, Paul does not tell us *how* to express the presence of God in our lives until the next verse: "Do not conform any longer to the pattern of this world, but be transformed by the renewing of your mind" (Romans 12:2a). When we live this way – always in God's presence – the result is declared in the latter part of the verse: "Then you will be able to test and approve what God's will is – his good, pleasing and perfect will" (Romans 12:2b).

The key to Paul's teaching in Romans 12:1-2 is that the presence of God within us and upon us motivates us to put off all that is worldly and put on all that will result in the transformation of our lives.

This admonition had a historical dimension in the first century that has the power to inform our personal journey in life. Let me explain.

When Christianity began it attracted a lot of gentiles – pagans with no moral training in what was good and evil. For example, abortion was as prevalent among them as it is today. They also committed infanticide without a sense of it being wrong. If a child they did not want was born to them, they simply took it to the woods and let it die. They basically lived without any kind of moral law or instruction. Hate, greed, violence, lust, and envy – to mention a few expressions of fallenness – were a way of life.

But when pagans became Christians, they were called to "turn away from evil" and "turn toward God." This is a turning toward all that is good, all that is of the Lord, all that is life-giving. As Paul states, "Be transformed by the renewing of your mind." For these new Christians, the church developed a form of instruction which appeared in lists of things to put off and lists of things to put on. These lists were associated with baptism. Baptism, as Paul teaches us in Romans 6:1-4, involves death to sin and being raised to a new life.

Baptism is an entrance into the death of Jesus. The old person – with all his/her sin, rebellion, and the old life of self-service – is drowned and brought to death. But baptism also represents a new way of life because it brings us into the resurrected life. Baptism is the symbol of our new life in Jesus. It calls us to put off the old and put on the new.

> *Whenever anyone asks me when I was saved, I always go back and describe my baptism. I was twelve when I was baptized. As I stood in the water, my father, the minister of the church, said: "Robert, do you renounce the devil and all his works?"*

> *I said, "I do." But I didn't even know all the works of the devil! Today, I know more of the devil's work, but I still don't know it all. After I have finished explaining my conversion and baptismal experience of saying "No" to the powers of evil and "Yes" to the powers of the Spirit in my life, I always say, "And I have been unpacking the meaning of my baptism all my life and hopefully will continue to do so as long as I live."*

Here is the Biblical pattern of spirituality. Spirituality is not a spiritual high or a warm fuzzy feeling; it is the actualization of putting off and putting on. Every time we put off a desire to sin, we enter into Jesus' death and drown the sin. Every time we choose that which is good and life-giving, we enter once again into the resurrection of Jesus and to the newness of life. This is the pattern of God's presence in our daily lives, a pattern that is to remain with us on a day-to-day, moment-by-moment basis.

Tertullian, a second century writer, knew this. Speaking of a heretical group he said, *"They full well know how to kill the little fishes, by taking them away from their water."*[1] In the water of baptism, God is present to assist us in our putting off and putting on. No wonder Martin Luther described the Christian life as "swimming in your baptismal waters."

Now let's go back again to the New Testament era and reflect on the teaching given to people who are candidates for baptism. The passages below have been identified by New Testament scholarship as pre-baptismal teachings on putting off the old and putting on the new.

First, note the teaching taking place in Rome: Here Paul uses the analogy of slavery and emphasizes how one is a slave to whatever or whomever one obeys (Romans 6:15-23).
You were slaves of unrighteousness...
- enslaved by impurity
- enslaved to ever increasing wickedness
- enslaved to sin; the wages of sin is death

You have become slaves of righteousness...
- enslaved to obedience, which leads to righteousness
- set free from sin
- enslaved to righteousness, which leads to holiness
- enjoying the results of eternal life; the gift of God is eternal life

---

[1] "On Baptism" in *The Ante-Nicene Fathers* Vol. 3 (Grand Rapids, Eerdmans, 1973) p. 669.

The teaching in Rome about putting off and putting on must have made a significant impact on the Roman Christians. They were able to say, "Well, if I'm going to let God's presence rest upon me and enter into my very being, I know what to do. I will behave in such a way that I will choose again and again to live a life that is no longer in obedience to unrighteousness. Instead I will choose the freedom of the new life by making myself a slave to righteousness." That message and that choice is as true today as it was in first-century Rome.

We also have the remnants of baptismal teaching used in the church of Colosse. Much of the book is oriented toward the rejection of the old and the embracing of the new, but we will look only at a portion of Colossians, chapters three and four. The baptismal theme is struck again when Paul says, "Set your minds on things above, not on earthly things" (Colossians 3:2). Then Paul draws on the instruction already known by the Colossians to make his point clear. He doesn't just give a general principle. He spells it out in these words: <u>Put to death, therefore, whatever belongs to your earthly nature</u>...

- sexual immorality
- impurity
- lust
- evil desires
- greed

<u>Now you must rid yourself of all such things as these:</u>
- anger
- rage
- malice
- slander
- filthy language
- lying to each other

You have taken off your old self with its practices and have put on the new self...
Therefore clothe yourself with:

- compassion
- kindness
- humility
- gentleness
- patience
- forbearance (with each other)
- forgiving whatever grievances you may have against one another
- forgiving as the Lord forgave you
- love
- the Word of Christ dwelling in you
- the singing of psalms, hymns, and spiritual songs
- devotion to prayer
- wisdom in the way you act toward outsiders
- gracious conversation

In addition, further specific instruction is given.

- Wives, submit to your husbands
- Husbands, love your wives
- Children, obey your parents
- Slaves (employees), obey your earthly masters
- Masters (employers), provide your employees with what is right

There is no missing of the moment in this pre-baptismal instruction. It is clear and unambiguous. It concentrates on specifics. It says that *when God's presence is upon you and in you, you live like a new person.*

109

The Galatian Christians also had a form of baptismal instruction that was familiar to the churches in that era. Paul heard that these Christians were struggling to understand how to live the new life. So Paul wrote to the Galatians to help them understand their pre-baptismal teaching. Paul was really clear, telling them this in summary: If you live in the old sinful way of all that is death, you put yourself in bondage to sin again. But if you turn your back on all that is death and embrace the life of the spirit, you will be empowered to live a whole new life in the freedom of the spirit. This instructional form is expressed in Galatians 5:16-26.

The sinful nature desires what is contrary to the spirit:
- sexual immorality
- impurity
- debauchery
- idolatry
- hatred
- discord
- jealousy
- fits of rage
- selfish ambition
- dissensions
- factions
- envy
- drunkenness
- orgies
- and the like

But the fruit of the spirit is:
- love
- joy
- peace
- patience
- kindness
- goodness

- faithfulness
- gentleness
- self control

New Christians in the Early Church didn't walk around asking, "So what should I be like now that I am a Christian?" For them it was abundantly clear that since the name of God was upon them, since they had been baptized into a death to the old way of life and a resurrection to the new way of life, they were called always to choose the way of the Spirit.

Even though the message of these pre-baptismal forms of instruction is 2000 years old, it is as pertinent today as it was then. We live in a pagan society where Christian values are rapidly disappearing. If we want to demonstrate God's presence upon us and within us, we must do so by our continual repentance from all that is sin and death in our lives, turning instead to all that is of the life-giving Spirit.

## Our Corporate Experience of the Presence of God in the Benediction

Biblical faith has always had both a personal dimension and a corporate dimension. For example: The Patriarchal Period emphasized the worship of the individual, whereas the Mosaic Era stressed the corporate community of people called to worship God.

What is true in Old Testament times is also true in the New Testament and in the era of the Church. God's presence rests on *me* as an individual Christian, but God's presence also abides within the community called Church. For that reason we must ask this question: How is the presence of God manifested in the Church as a corporate people functioning in the world?

**111**

The most crucial image in the New Testament that teaches the presence of Jesus in the Church is that of "the body of Christ" (I Corinthians 12:1-31). In theological terms the Church is the continuation of the incarnation. It is the necessary dimension of Jesus in the world. It is the sign of God's presence in the world. Therefore, it is to serve as salt and light within the world.

Numerous books have been written on the subject of the Church in the world. One of the best is an early description given to us by an anonymous author in the second century. The writing is called the *Epistle to Diognetus*,[1] and the author clearly spells out how God's presence in the corporate body of the Church is expressed in the corporate life of God's people. The author makes three key statements:

First of all, he wants to make it abundantly clear that Christians are not weird offbeats, but like all other people in the world they live lives that are quite normal within the culture of the day. Consequently, according to the writer, "Christians cannot be distinguished from the rest of the human race by country, language or customs. They do not live in cities of their own; they do not use a peculiar form of speech; and they do not follow an eccentric manner of life" (Letter to Diognetus 5:1-3).

Next the writer wants to show how Christians who have the presence of God upon them are different, so he writes, "They marry, like everyone else, and they beget children, but they do not cast off their offspring. They share their board with each other, but not their marriage bed" (5:6-7). The author goes on to say, "They busy themselves on earth, but their

---

[1]This epistle is contained in its entirety in Cyril Richardson, *Early Christian Fathers* (Philadelphia: Westminster Press) pp. 213-224.

citizenship is in heaven. They obey the established laws, but in their own lives they go far beyond what the laws require" (5:9-10).

The third image given to us by this anonymous author is most compelling. It moves from what Christians *are not* to what Christians *are*. "To put it simply," the author states, "what the soul is in the body, that Christians are in the world" (6:1).

Here is an absolutely radical concept of the presence of God in the world. The Church, the corporate body of Jesus Christ, is to the world what the soul is to the body. The Church is the interior personality of the world. The world has not been forsaken by God; instead, God has entrusted His presence in the world to the Church.

How does this idea translate into the work of the Church in the world? Unfortunately, there are many who feel this means that the Church is to rule the world through political involvement. "If only," some people say, "we could get committed Christians into every level of government, then we could change the world."

The concept of political change through a Christian political presence in the governments of the world was never taught by Jesus, by the apostles, or by the Early Church.

Indeed the Church is understood to be political, but not political in the ways of the world. Rather *the Church is called to live by the politics of the Kingdom,* a politics not of this world, but of the One who in the end will rule and reign over the whole world.

What does this mean? It means that the Church in its corporate nature is the sign of the Kingdom to come. As a sign of the Kingdom it is already the new creation of God being formed in the midst of all that is old and subject to death.

Therefore the Church is a counterculture community. It is, at its very core, different from the fallen community which surrounds it. Its work in the world is to be the presence of God, the place where God's name is worshiped; the place where God's rules for living in the spirit are obeyed; the place where one can look and say, *"God dwells here."*

## Bringing Stage Four into Focus

Like Cleopas who went forth having met the presence of God at Word and Table, we too want to be transformed and empowered to tell others and to live the new life. Telling others does not mean jamming Christ down someone's throat in an aggressive and controlling way. Telling others is a natural response of our everyday living.

> *For example, I was on a plane recently and the man next to me noticed I was reading a Christian book. He asked me about the book and about what I do, and soon we were involved in a full-blown, animated discussion about religion. He was a Buddhist and was attempting to help me get a grasp on his point of view. I asked, "Can you tell me in one line or so what Buddhism says?"*
>
> *His response was this: "Buddhism says we are all part of the problem and all part of the solution."*
>
> *We went on to discuss what this meant in terms of the problem of evil and the ultimate destiny of*

114

*humanity. After a while I said, "I'd like to share
with you what lies at the heart of Christianity."*

*"Please do," he said. "I'm quite interested."*

*Here was my statement:*
*"Christianity recognizes the problem of evil in which
we are all involved, but it emphasizes that one man
— Jesus Christ — solved for us all, by taking our
place, the problem we could never solve for ourselves."
This was a subtle form of communication that
hopefully set up within this stranger a phrase, an
idea that he could mull over in his heart. He heard
the truth — not all of it, but enough to open a crack
to let the Christian light enter his heart.*

Telling others is also the work of the corporate church. Here,
for example is a story told to me by Tommy Coombs, leader
of the *Maranatha! Band*:

*"You know Bob, I was a hippie back in the late 60's,
but I was a hippie looking for God and peace in my
life. I tried everything, but nothing clicked. My life
was one great big hole of meaninglessness. Then one
day somebody said to me, "Hey, Tommy! Why don't
you come with me to Calvary Church in Costa Mesa?
That's where you will find God, for God dwells there
in that church."*

*Tommy continued, "You know, Bob, the moment I
opened the door of the church, saw the people, and
heard the singing, I knew I was home. I knew that
God dwelt there."*

His life was radically transformed because he was

115

encountered by the presence of God expressed in the worship of Calvary Church.

This is possible for every person and every church. God's presence dwells in us and we, in the Church, dwell in the world as the soul to the body.

Live in such a way that your new life transforms others as well.

## How Far Have We Come?

- We have been gathered, instructed, nourished, and now desire to share with others
- We are energized and anointed through the benediction, the blessing
- We are reminded that we are not alone in this journey – God is with us
- We are baptized to put off the old life and put on the new life
- We recognize that we are the Body of Christ, revealing Him to the world

## Thinking It Over

1) Describe any incident in your life which was so powerful and meaningful to you that you had to tell someone about it right away.
2) Tell your own story of faith as you would comunicate it to a friend.
3) How would you use the image of baptism to explain to someone else the power of Christ to change a life?

# ostscript: Our Journey into the Presence of God

*"They stayed continually at the temple, praising God"*
*(Luke 24:53).*

It has been my purpose throughout this book to focus on our journey of worship and to pay special attention to those ways in which God becomes present in personal and public worship.

Now it is time for us to reflect on the whole process and resolve to enter more fully into the presence of God through our journey. I have been thinking about that for myself, since I am primarily a worshiper and only secondarily a writer and teacher in worship.

An important reflection, and one that I have mentioned frequently throughout this book, is always to remember that *God initiates worship. We respond.* In talking to people about worship, I frequently hear a language of worship legalism. "I am the one who has to work up the emotion and fervor, then God will come to me." I'm not exactly sure where that error comes from, but it is not Biblical and it is certainly debilitating for the worshiper. It puts the worshiper under tremendous performance pressure. Either he feels he must exaggerate his or her experience or be downright dishonest about feelings in worship. I have found it to be wonderfully freeing to know

117

that the reality and significance of worship is primarily the work of God and only secondarily my response.

## God's Work

Let's focus first on the primacy of the work of God in worship. The Greek word *leitourgia* is the root word for worship. It means work or ministry. In the New Testament it refers to the work and ministry of the Temple priests (Luke 1:23), to the heavenly work of Christ (Hebrews 8:6), to the work and ministry of the church (Acts 13:2), and to Christian service and ministry in general (Romans 15:27; II Corinthians 9:12; Philippians 2:7).

But what is this work, this ministry, this service to God? We see in the story of Cleopas the fourfold pattern for private and public worship:

- It is to gather in God's presence;
- to hear God speak to us of His great saving deeds by which He has called us out of darkness into His marvelous light (I Peter 2:9)
- to respond with praise and thanksgiving, especially with the symbols of His great work for us, the bread and wine;
- to go forth into the world to love and serve the Lord.

There are, of course many things we *do* in worship which express our desire to serve and minister to God: We bow down, we fall before, we venerate, we humble ourselves, we acknowledge, we submit. But all these actions of worship are secondary to the primary purpose of worship which is *the work of rehearsing and strengthening the relationship that exists between God and the church. This is a relationship which God initiated and which God sustains, continually calling us to*

**118**

*gather to deepen our understanding of this unique relationship, and to resolve to go forth to live it out in life as a sign of God's presence in the world.*

That's the divine side of worship.

## My/Our Response

But the work of God in worship also demands a response. We do not treat the rehearsal of our relationship with God in a ho-hum fashion. Instead, we are to engage in a full, active, and conscious participation. There are several ways we can achieve a more intense participation in worship.

First, a primary attitude for all of us is to go to worship with a *"broken and contrite heart"* (Psalm 51:17). When we go to worship with a proud or haughty attitude, we erect barriers to the rehearsal of God's great deeds of salvation taking any effect in our lives. We continually need to ask God to change us, to melt our hearts of stone, to break us from the inside. This is not a once-in-a-while prayer but a continual repentance on our part.

We are led to the recognition that *all of worship is prayer*. We do have within worship specific kinds of prayers – invocations, intercessory prayers, and prayers of thanksgiving – but all of worship is a prayer. Prayer is a relationship, an act of communication, a union with the divine. From the start of the Gathering of the assembly to the Benediction, worship is about a union (a prayer) with the God who *journeys* us into His presence. The error of entertainment worship lies in the fact that it is too reminiscent of our secular culture. It's a plateful of the same stuff we get in the world. It's Christianity wrapped up in contemporary, pop-culture dress. No wonder it's not satisfying!

119

Celebrating worship as a prayer connects us with the record of God's "hound of heaven" search for us. It unites us with all other Christians around the world and with two thousand years of history in which God's people have consciously prayed through the relationship God has made with us. In this prayer, the content of God's saving action takes up residence within us.

For this reason we need to go to worship with *intention*. There are always two sides to a relationship. What is true in the human arena is true in the divine as well. Worship is a meeting between the divine and the human. God has made us with the power of choice. God wants us to choose what God has done for us in history to redeem us and to restore us. But we do have to choose it through intention. We want to do what God wants to do in worship.

Intentional worship will eventuate in *attentiveness*. All good relationships include paying attention to each other. Worship is a conversation with God. God calls us to worship; God communicates to us in the Word; God asks for our response of praise and thanksgiving; and God sends us forth. If we are indifferent to this conversation, it is like never listening to a spouse, children, parents, or a favored friend. The one difference is that these people may give up and go away, but God is characterized by steadfastness.

Even if you quit attending church — where God establishes, maintains, repairs, and transforms relationship — God will not leave you alone. He will come to you: through creation, through incidents in your life, through unexpected circumstances. He will say again and again, *"My child, I'm talking to you... are you listening?"* Learn to listen in worship. Listen to the sounds of worship; listen to the atmosphere of worship; listen to the voice of God in worship. This doesn't happen automatically. It happens through an intentional commitment that rises first by your conscious choice to listen. Eventually the art of listening will take root in your heart and will occur more naturally.

If we listen, we will be led into *praise and thanksgiving*. Praise and thanksgiving have always been a response to the Word, a response that thanks God for the work of the Son to redeem and save the world. Unfortunately, in the twofold pattern of worship and teaching, our worship leaders design worship to be praise and thanksgiving first, then the Word. As we can see from the Biblical record, this has turned worship inside out. Unless we are careful we can miss the point of gathering, in that although we do gather, we often don't realize the divine and human dynamic. Then, because we neglect the Eucharist, we don't have an appropriate context in which we do our thanksgiving. We may have to change our worship order and rethink what we do in order to achieve a more Biblical experience of thanksgiving.

Finally, we need to worship with *resolve*. In worship, God is forming His own people, His own peculiar possession in the world (I Peter 2:9-10). By the constant rehearsal of God's covenantal relationship with us and in us, we are called to Christ-likeness. This does not happen automatically, simply because we are present at the worship event where we are told what kind of person and community God wants to spread over the whole earth. It happens for us when we resolve to live the life and to be the *ecclesia* (called-out ones) in a world that desperately needs the presence of God fully alive in the Church.

## But I Can't Do It!
I have just outlined a tall demand. Go to worship with a broken heart; make all your worship a prayer; be intentional

in every aspect of worship, by being attentive to the rehearsal of your relationship with God, by offering praise and thanksgiving; and resolve to live as a child of the king.

There are two things about this demand that we need to grasp: The first is that we *can* do it; the second is that we *can't* do it.

First, God wants our full, conscious, and active participation in worship. We can't brush true worship aside in favor of dead ritualism or indifference. True worship involves relationship, and that takes work (*Leitourgia*). Worship is the work of the people, and we are called to see worship as a vocation. It is not our vacation, our rest time, our down time. It is our work, as in our calling before God. We are to do it as passionately as we would enter into any enjoyable and compelling relationship.

## Jesus Has Done It

Try as we might, we really can't *perfectly* do what I've suggested above. Even though God's people are redeemed, they are not perfect. So we will never achieve the fullness of a broken heart, or of worship as prayer, or of intention, or of attentiveness, or of praise and thanksgiving, or of resolve. Our fallen nature always stands in the way.

God knows that, so He does not demand perfect worship from you and me. Instead God became incarnate in Jesus Christ to do, in the same humanity which He shares with us, what we cannot do for ourselves.

God became incarnate so that the human nature which we received from Adam might be restored, redeemed, and transformed. Jesus is the second Adam. He perfectly repre-

122

sents us to the Father. He, Jesus in His human nature, *is* our broken and contrite heart. He *is* our continual prayer; He *is* perfect intention; He *is* our attention. His very life, death, and resurrection is an offering of praise and thanksgiving which He presents on our behalf.

Jesus is our heavenly liturgist (Hebrews 8:6) and we, united to His perfect human nature, are through Him united to God. We are free to worship in the best way we know how, offering our feeble attempts to God, always knowing that what we do is not enough, but confident that what Jesus has done is all that is needed!

If that's good enough for God, it's good enough for me. "I trust then not in myself, but in Jesus."

I think we have just worshiped.

Thanks be to God!

## Thinking It Over

1) Describe a recent experience of worship in terms of your *intention,* your *attentiveness,* your *praise and thanksgiving*, and your *resolve*.
2) Reread the final two sections "But, I Can't Do It" and "Jesus Has Done It." What kind of response does this create in your heart?

# *Bibliography*

Borgen, Ole E., *John Wesley on the Sacraments* ( Nashville: Abington Press, 1972).

Jasper, R.C.D., and Cummings, G.J., eds. *Prayers of the Eucharist: Early and Reformed,* 2nd Ed. (New York: Oxford University Press, 1980).

*Lutherworks,* vol. 37, *Word and Sacrament III* (Philadelphia: Mohlenberg Press, 1961).

Richardson, Cyril, *Early Christian Fathers* (Philadelphia: Westminster Press, 1963).

Tertullian "On Baptism" in *The Ante-Nicene Fathers* vol. 3 (Grand Rapids: Eerdmans, 1973).

124

# The Institute for Worship Studies

## The Three Arms of IWS

### Worship Education

There are three arms to the work of IWS. The first is the IWS education arm. We offer the D. Min. in worship in partnership with Northern Baptist Theological Seminary in Lombard, Illinois (near Chicago). We also offer the Doctor of Worship Studies (DWS) for qualified music ministers and worship leaders at our Jacksonville, Florida campus. In partnership with Tyndale Theological Seminary in Toronto we also offer an M. T.S. in worship. We also offer a Certificate For Worship Studies (CWS) for lay persons and others who are not able to take one of our degree programs. This program consists of seven long-distance courses that are taken in the convenience of the home and according to the desired pace of the student.

All degree courses are taught as intensives in January, June, and August of each year. All IWS faculty are adjunct professors who have a doctorate in worship studies and have worked in the field of worship in post-doctoral studies. While each scholar is committed to academic research, each is also deeply committed to the relevance of academia to worship renewal in the local church.

125

## Worship Resources

Our second arm is to make pertinent books and audio and video resources available to the local church. These materials are all characterized by strong Biblical and historical scholarship and relevance. We carry more than 30 useful products.

## Worship Workshops

Our third arm is the sponsoring of one-day educational events on worship called *Renew Your Worship!* These seminars provide information and inspiration for local pastors and worship leaders. We do about 30 seminars a year with approximately three to five thousand people in attendance. All workshops are done in person by Robert Webber.

# *Other Books and Resources on Worship by the Author*

## I.  Reference Work:

*The Complete Library of Christian Worship* 7 vols.
(Peabody: Hendrickson, 1993-1995) volumes are:
   *The Biblical Foundations of Christian Worship*
   *Twenty Centuries of Christian Worship*
   *The Renewal of Sunday Worship*
   *Music and the Arts in Christian Worship* (volumes A & B)
   *The Christian Year*
   *The Sacred Actions of Christian Worship*
   *The Ministries of Christian Worship*


## II. Books for personal or group study (all published by Hendrickson)
(The IWS Certificate of Worship Studies is based on the study of these books)

*Learning To Worship With All Your Heart: A Study in the
   Biblical Foundations of Worship,* 1996
*Rediscovering The Missing Jewel:   A Study in Twenty
   Centuries of Christian Worship,* 1997
*Renew Your Worship! A Study in Blending Traditional and
   Contemporary Worship,* 1997
*Enter His Court With Praise: A Study of Music and the
   Arts in Worship,* 1998
*Rediscovering The Christian Feasts: A Study in the Services
   of the Christian Year,* 1998

127

*Encountering The Healing Power Of God: A Study in the Sacred Action of Worship,* 1998

*Empowered By The Holy Spirit: A Study in the Ministries of Worship,* 1998

## III. Resources for understanding and planning worship

*Worship Old and New* (Grand Rapids: Zondervan, 1994)
*Worship Is a Verb* (Peabody: Hendrickson, 1985)
*Planning Blended Worship* (Nashville: Abingdon, 1998)
*Blended Worship* (Peabody: Hendrickson, 1992)

## IV. Resources for worship and outreach

*Liturgical Evangelism* (Harrisburg: Morehouse, 1992)
*People of the Truth* (Harrisburg: Morehouse, 1993)

## V. Resources for worship and spirituality

*The Praise and Worship Study Bible* (Carol Stream: TyndalePress, 1997).
*The Book of Daily Prayer* (Grand Rapids: Eerdmans, 1993).
*The Book of Family Prayer* (Peabody: Hendrickson, 1996).

## VI. Audio Resources

*Blended Worship* (Wheaton: IWS, 1996)
   *The Original Renew Your Worship Workshop! Blending Traditional and Contemporary Worship*

128

## VII. Music Resource

*Renew! Songs and Hymns For Blended Worship* (Carol Stream: Hope Publishers, 1996) Available in three editions: Accompaniment ring binder, soft cover melody edition, and hard cover melody edition.

## All Resources Are Available through IWS

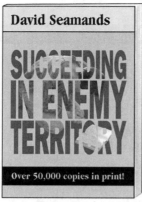

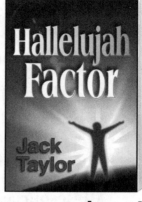

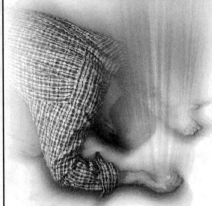

# Discover the keys to effective prayer and intercession!

Intercessors, prayer warriors, and praying Christians everywhere are discovering prayer in a fresh, powerful way. *Prayer Audio Magazine*™ will catapult your prayer and intercession to new levels.

God desires to communicate intimately with you through prayer. Through *Prayer Audio Magazine* you can invite the world's leading authorities into your own home to help you pray with greater effectiveness.

Each audio cassette has been prayerfully developed to help you maximize your prayer life.

Be more effective. Be informed. Pray with greater fervency and power! Get the best of *Prayer Audio Magazine* today!

## The best of Prayer Audio Magazine:

- 12 audio cassettes featuring the world's leading authorities on prayer and intercession – these are 12 of the best issues ever of *Prayer Audio Magazine*
- 12 helpful listening guides (one for each cassette)
- Deluxe storage binder stores all 12 cassettes and listening guides
- Exclusive interviews and more
- Noted speakers include: Judson Cornwall, C. Peter Wagner, and Eddie & Alice Smith

*"Prayer Audio Magazine challenges us to keep pressing in to God. It keeps us informed, and brings us together to bond in prayer..."*
– Pastor Jim Ottman, Maine

**Only ~~$97~~ $87** with coupon or special code on coupon **+ $9.97 shipping**
60-Day Money Back Guarantee

**Call toll free (800) 597-1123**

## SAVE $10

With this coupon, you can get the best of *Prayer Audio Magazine* for only $87!

*Just mention special* Code #PUBS108 *to receive your $10 off!*

# AMBP

**1-800-597-1123**

P.O. Box 486
Mansfield, PA 16933

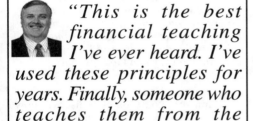

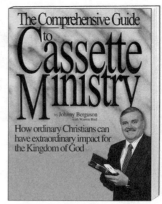

# Get the only Bible on Cassette that you can copy and give away

Suddenly you can give copies of the New Testament on Cassette to friends. Make a copy for your school. Copy several for your outreach ministry.

Or copy it for any ministry reason you want and give it away – you won't pay one cent in royalty fees! (We just ask that you don't copy the tapes for resale or profit.) Never before has anyone, anywhere made the Bible on cassette so easily available to so many.

Two years of planning was put into this Bible on Cassette before any production started.

## Unique features of The Classic℠ King James Version

- The only Bible on Cassette you can copy and give away!
- 16 Free Access℠ studio quality master cassettes of the New Testament
- Recorded at the perfect speed for comprehension and enjoyment (It's not jam-packed onto 12 cassettes to save money)
- Digitally recorded to prevent listener fatigue
- Features the phenomenal voice of Dr. Vernon Lapps

16 Master Cassettes of the New Testament

### The Classic℠ King James Version Bible on Cassette

narrated by Dr. Vernon Lapps

**ISBN: 1-883906-14-8** **Only $47.00**

Code #PUBS108

# Discover how ordinary Christians can multiply the effectiveness of their whole church!

*"This book was so good I could hardly put it down. This book showed me how to do everything... plus it's an abundant source of ideas. I thank God for putting this book in my hands. And I truly believe cassette ministry is a God given tool..."*
– Carol Faust, Florida

As you catch the vision for cassette ministry, you'll quickly discover how to help make your entire church more effective through cassette ministry.

That's right. Anyone, anywhere can help make their ENTIRE church more effective through cassette ministry. You won't find another book like this anywhere!

*The Comprehensive Guide to Cassette Ministry* is loaded with practical ideas that will help you increase the effectiveness of nearly every ministry in your church. You'll discover four compelling Biblical reasons to do cassette ministry, the right – and wrong – ways to do it; how to fund your tape ministry; how to increase evangelism, teaching, and pastoral care through cassettes. You'll learn everything you could possibly want to know.

This book is helping ordinary Christians everywhere help make their entire church more effective!

### The Comprehensive Guide to Cassette Ministry by Johnny Berguson

**ISBN: 1-883906-12** **Only $19.97**

Code #PUBS108

## Available at your local Christian bookstore or call toll free (800) 597-1123